HAVENS

IN A

HECTIC WORLD

HAVENS

IN A

HECTIC WORLD

Finding Sacred Places

Star Weiss

TouchWood Editions
#108 – 17665 66A Avenue
Surrey, BC V3S 2A7
www.touchwoodeditions.com

TouchWood Editions
PO Box 468
Custer, WA
98240-0468

LIBRARY AND ARCHIVES CANADA CATALOGUING IN PUBLICATION

Weiss, Star, 1948–
        Havens in a hectic world : finding sacred places / Star Weiss.

    Includes bibliographical references.

        1. Peace of mind. 2. Sacred space—British Columbia. 3. Self-actualization (Psychology). I. Title.

    BF637.P3W43 2008   158   C2008-900289-X

LIBRARY OF CONGRESS CONTROL NUMBER: 2008921285

Edited by Marlyn Horsdal
Cover and book design by Val Speidel
Chapter title illustrations: Joanne Thomson, © CRCC 2007
Author photo: Farah Nosh
All photographs by Star Weiss, unless otherwise noted.
Portions of this book, and several of the images, have appeared, sometimes in different versions, in "Sacred Places" columns in *Focus, Victoria's Monthly Magazine of People, Ideas and Culture*, between 2005 and 2007, and in "A Place Apart," *Shared Vision*, December 2004.
Page ii: Cathedral Grove; pages vi–vii: Tofino; page x: Cox Bay, Tofino

TouchWood Editions acknowledges the financial support for its publishing program from the Government of Canada through the Book Publishing Industry Development Program (BPIDP), Canada Council for the Arts, and the Province of British Columbia through the British Columbia Arts Council and the Book Publishing Tax Credit.

To Sharon Hall,
my friend who left this world during the writing of this book,

and to Sophia Emily Broadland,
my granddaughter who entered this world during
the same time

CONTENTS

FOREWORD

by Jo-Ann Roberts

O N A RECENT TRIP to the United Nations headquarters in New York, I visited the Meditation Room. It is a small, unadorned, quiet room just off the main lobby. Amidst the hustle and bustle of ambassadors and security guards, media crews and tourists, it's easy to miss this little oasis of peace if you're not looking for it.

The room was created by Dag Hammarskjold when he was Secretary General. On a plaque just outside the door are the words he wrote to explain its significance:

"We all have within us a centre of stillness surrounded by silence. This house, dedicated to work and debate in the service of peace, should have one room dedicated to silence in the outward sense and stillness in the inner sense. A place where the doors may be open to the infinite lands of thought and prayer."

Thanks to my friendship and recent collaboration with Star Weiss, I feel I can appreciate the universal truth of these words by Hammarskjold. While I was raised in an active Christian home and considered myself to be a spiritual person interested in matters of faith, until a fateful conversation with Star two years ago, I really hadn't given much thought to the places where we find solace and healing—places where we can open the doors to "the infinite lands of thought and prayer."

My husband and I were visiting Star and her husband, Russ, one evening when the conversation turned to a series of columns Star was writing on people and their sacred places. Over a glass of wine we started sharing stories of places that had been sacred in our lives. We could have talked all night. On another visit, Star told me she was now working on a book and I invited her to talk about it on the afternoon radio show that I host. The interview went well and as a result other journalists became interested in Star's work on this subject.

Over the next few months, whenever Star and I were together she would share new stories. My interest now became more than just a growing personal awareness of the sacred. As a radio journalist, I longed to hear the voices of these people, their stories. I wanted to go on an audio journey to their sacred places.

Star's enthusiasm for this topic is infectious. She inspired me to take my idea for a radio documentary on sacred places and make it a reality. Once we had the necessary approval for a two-hour national radio special, we were faced with a time crunch, about three weeks to record interviews, write, edit and compile our show. We were able to get our guests quickly because many of them already knew Star. Their willingness to tell their stories again on tape for the country to hear was a tribute to their faith in her. Many of their stories are in this book, and there were other people I had met through my work whom I felt would be willing to share their stories. We were also granted permission to record the stories of First Nations inmates at William Head Institution.

In the process of putting the show together, I found something Star had discovered when she was told she had breast cancer: I found my own sacred spaces and explored what they have meant to me. As part of the show, we had both agreed to tell our own stories of where we go to find healing and peace. I had been to Star's writer's hut and the beach where she and Russ go to feel the presence of the divine in their lives, and I started looking for these places in my own life. I am at peace when I see the red soil of Prince Edward Island, or sit next to the ocean and watch the waves, or pray in the quiet of ancient cathedrals. I have learned to listen for the "still, small voice of God."

What I hope you will find in this book is the inspiration to tell your own stories of healing and sacred places. And that these stories will encourage you to see the world differently and know there is value in finding your centre of stillness and surrounding it with silence.

Jo-Ann Roberts
Host, *All Points West*, CBC Radio One

Map 1: Haida Gwaii / Queen Charlotte Islands

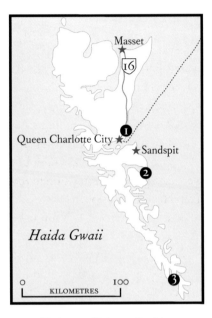

Masset
16
Queen Charlotte City
Sandspit
1
2
Haida Gwaii
0   100
KILOMETRES
3

1 Skidegate (Balance Rock)
2 Skedans (K'una)
3 Ninstints (SGaang Gwaii)

Map 2: Vancouver Island and the Sunshine Coast

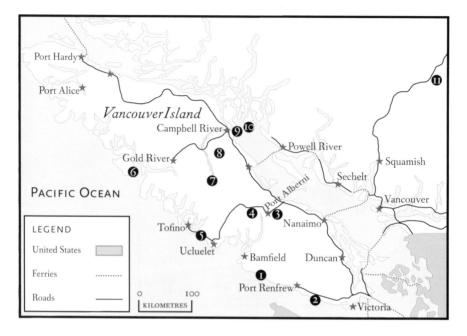

Port Hardy
Port Alice
Vancouver Island
Campbell River
Gold River
Powell River
Squamish
Sechelt
Port Alberni
Vancouver
PACIFIC OCEAN
Tofino
Nanaimo
Ucluelet
Bamfield
Duncan
Port Renfrew
Victoria

LEGEND

United States	
Ferries	....
Roads	————

0   100
KILOMETRES

1   Carmanah Walbran Provincial Park
2   Sombrio Beach
3   Cathedral Grove
4   Sproat Lake
5   Long Beach
6   Yuquot (Friendly Cove)
7   Myra Falls
8   Mt. Albert Edward
9   Quadra Island United Church
10 Hollyhock
11 Whistler (Village Church)

Map 3: Vancouver and the Lower Mainland

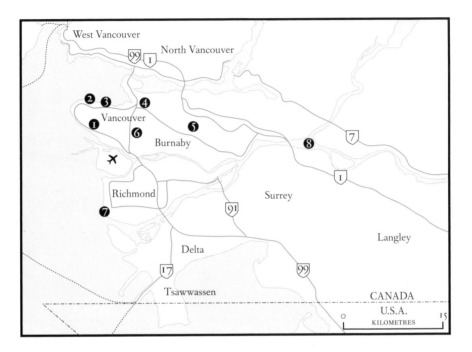

1   Pacific Spirit Park
2   Locarno Beach
3   Jericho Beach
4   Downtown Eastside, Vancouver (Saint Paul's Parish)
5   Ismaili Jamatkhana, Burnaby
6   Unitarian Church, Vancouver
7   Garry Point (Steveston)
8   Fraser River

Map 4: Victoria and Southern Vancouver Island

1 Glenairley
2 Witty's Lagoon Regional Park
3 William Head (Institution)
4 Tower Point
5 Ogden Point
6 Victoria (cherry blossoms)
7 Christ Church Cathedral (labyrinth)
8 Victoria Hospice
9 Synagogue (Congregation Emanu-El)
10 Queenswood
11 Interfaith Chapel (University of Victoria)
12 Gordon Head
13 Francis/King Regional Park
14 LA'UWELN̲EW̲
15 YAAS Mountain
16 Shawnigan Creek
17 Sylvan United Church
18 Reginald Hill (Trail)
19 Central Cemetery
20 Burgoyne Bay Provincial Park
21 Providence Farm
22 St. Clare's Monastery

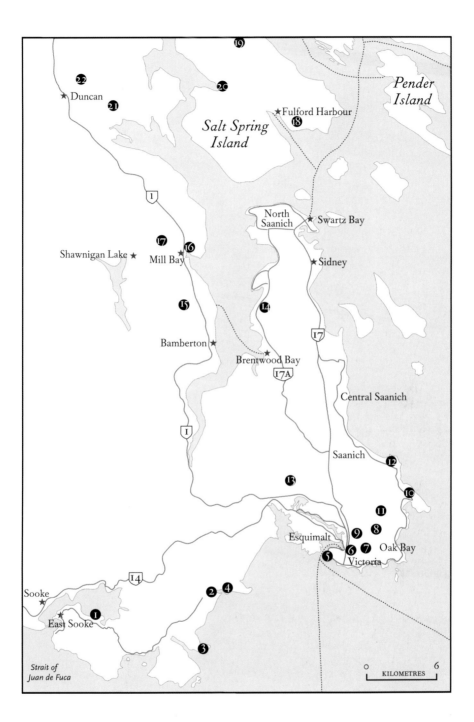

The Sacred Where of the British Columbia Coast

->->->-<-<-<-

*In belonging to a landscape, one feels a rightness,
at-homeness, a knitting of self and world.*

SCOTT RUSSELL SANDERS, in *Staying Put*

->-<-

O NE CLEAR October night, my husband, Russ Fuoco, and I joined a group of people who had gathered quietly on the front lawn of the provincial legislature in Victoria. We had come, like everyone else, to light and place a luminary on the grass to honour those we have lost to and those who are surviving cancer. Rows of glowing paper lanterns, a name inscribed on each, illuminated the normally dark expanse. We walked slowly, past strangers in tears, stopping to read each inscription: "To Mommy. I miss you." "To Dad." "To my best buddy."

The lawn became a sacred site that evening, graced by the ritual of remembrance, the people silently but emotionally linked to each other and to something

◄ Candles on the Lawn ceremony. The lawn of the provincial legislature in Victoria, BC, became a sacred site that night. PHOTO BY MEGHAN BLANCHARD

beyond themselves. The beauty of those points of light, the shared realization that this honouring was something holy, created sacredness in that very public place.

Sacred places are sometimes found in unexpected locations and can be created by us almost anywhere we bring a certain—what? Why do some circumstances affect us this way? What makes a place sacred? We may know it when we feel it but still not be able to describe it. What elements combine, both externally in our surroundings and internally in our hearts and minds, to bring about this aura, this sense of hallowed ground? Is it intentionality? Remembrance? Beauty? Pain? Communality? Perhaps a sacred place is anywhere we feel a communion—an intimate fellowship—with others.

The Candles on the Lawn ceremony was particularly meaningful to us that night because I had recently completed treatment for breast cancer myself. And going through that personal crisis was like going through a sieve that strained out the chunky clutter of daily routine and left behind only the essential ingredients. It compressed the slow-burning coal of my life into the white-hot core of my being, in one superheated thrust.

This is definitely life-altering, but it is not all bad. It tended to make me take a closer, more appreciative look at the people and places in my life. I felt, with a new pinprick of urgency, that I was unfinished in my quest of trying to figure out how God, faith and all the big questions of existence fit into my West Coast existence. I wanted to know more about the people who live here, and how they are finding the sacred in their lives. I started asking the questions, and found that for many, their interludes of soulfulness are connected to a sacred place.

For years I've believed that the power of place—that is, the spiritual geography—of British Columbia amounts to a religious force that affects how we see the world, what we believe and how we come to terms with faith and spirituality. So, I've been taking a closer look at the *genius loci* (spirit of place) here in BC. I've been going to locations up and down the coast that seem, to me or to others, to have a sacred quality that resonates, like a tuning fork twanging in our hearts.

I guess it's not surprising that the universal search for meaning in our lives often begins with a journey, the act of seeking transcendence or transformation simply by going somewhere significant. Pilgrims have been searching for the path to the Creator or the link to the divine, an experience of oneness with the Earth, for centuries. Now, in the multi-tasking mélange that most of us call everyday life, we seem to need this assurance of a sacred place more than ever.

Maybe that's because so many other footholds in our society have been eroded as we emerge into a time of change, when the familiar way our society has been organized—around religion, family, state—seems to be in flux. The old is often gone, but the new is only beginning to emerge. We look for something tangible to hold onto, literally, as we make our way through our lives, and a place, especially a place on the West Coast, is often the touchstone we need.

-+>-<+-

WHEN I MOVED to British Columbia from New York State in 1972, the natural beauty and resource-based, earthy lifestyle of this glorious part of the world smacked me in the face. I was captivated by the fact that so many people here worked in primary industry, right on the land—felling trees, catching fish, extracting minerals, directly and daily in contact with the resources of Mother Earth. I was familiar with secondary industry at best, or administrative offices far removed from the raw (and to this day often dangerous) physicality of jobs in logging, fishing or mining. It was a heady experience to be living in a resource-based economy, in the midst of some of the wildest and most dramatic landscapes I had ever seen. It caused a shift in my world view, I realize now, and set me up for the next stage of my spiritual quest

Once displaced, I, like the early white settlers to BC, felt free to start over, discard old notions and come up with a new way of seeing the world and the big questions that come with it. And I began to notice something: I was influenced by the grandeur and proximity of the natural world in a way that, growing up in the eastern United States, had never been part of my experience. I noticed that

other BC residents, whether born here or immigrants like me, were also affected by what author Kathleen Norris refers to as "spiritual geography, the way a place shapes people's attitudes, beliefs, myths."[1]

And taking a big leap (but I think there is some truth to it, as least in my own observations), those endless, navel-gazing, meaning-of-life-God-and-the-universe discussions of my earlier eastern life were often missing, replaced by soul-stirring firsthand observations of divine grandeur that I experienced while standing on mountaintops, walking on windswept beaches, hiking among the biggest trees I'd ever seen or sitting quietly on a hilltop gazing at the display of spring wildflowers.

My BC-born-and-bred husband, Russ, and I started our family while we were living in an old fisherman's cottage on Quadra Island, across from Campbell River on Vancouver Island. Here, I was first introduced to the rich Kwakiutl (now referred to as Kwagiulth, or in this case specifically, We-Wai-Kai) culture of the coast. A unique phenomenon of Quadra life at that time was the flourishing Quadra Island United Church, where the people of the We-Wai-Kai band on the Cape Mudge reserve were joined by islanders from all parts of the island for services on Sunday evenings.

Our minister was Ron Atkinson, a poet-philosopher who gave "sermons" that were artistically crafted meditations on life and led us in services that were odes to the joys of island living: that is, to the truths of the universe as reflected

◄ Hiking the ridge to First Brother, Manning Park, BC.

in our microscopic piece of the world. The elders of the church were elders of the Cape Mudge band, and this confluence of Native and non-Native voices is, I later learned, unusual. At the time, I knew only that this felt right, that I was enriched and expanded by the coming together of the Quadra community in one inclusive, authentic psalm. I didn't know enough to realize how rare this was, but to this day the church at Cape Mudge is one of my sacred places.

A few years later, we moved to Maple Bay, on the fringes of Duncan, BC. I started working for the Cowichan Valley Intercultural and Immigrant Aid Society, and I became actively involved in the multicultural, multi-faith community that is also a part of the fabric of this province. Moving into another stage of my own spiritual journey, I became much more aware of the beliefs of new Canadians coming from a wide spectrum of religious backgrounds: Sikhs, Jews, Muslims, Christians, Buddhists, Baha'is and Hindus, among others.

I began teaching First Nations adults in a job re-entry program at the Native Friendship Centre (Hiiye'yu Lelum) in Duncan, and began to learn more about First Nations spirituality from my students and colleagues. I was invited into the longhouse, observed and took part in Quw'utsun ceremonies and listened to elders.

Over the years, my childhood habits of weekly church attendance and faithful involvement in all aspects of the social fellowship of a church congregation fell away. Part of me is sorry about this, and still misses it. Another part of me knows that I am looking now for something different, even though I'm still trying to figure out exactly what that "something" is.

And I don't think I'm alone in this. We live in a time of transition, when our institutions often no longer meet our needs. In most parts of Canada, and many parts of the United States, church attendance in the mainstream churches, historically the backbone of the religious life of North America, has fallen dramatically in the last 30 years. Here in BC, the decline is more startling than anywhere else on the continent. I wanted to know more about how and where we are finding the sacred in the 21st century, especially on the West Coast, a long-time hotbed for all things leading-edge and non-traditional.

As baby boomers get to the more reflective phase of their lives, the search for meaning becomes both wider and deeper. I think we each want to find our place in the universe, literally. Where do we fit in the world? What part do we play?

After my experience with cancer, those questions seemed even more pressing to me. I began to realize that one way we each find our place in the macrocosm in which we live is to first find our place in the more manageable microcosm of our personal lives.

I've also realized that other people are wonderful mentors and guides, and each person I have met on my journey has added another bit of refracted light to the kaleidoscope I looked through as I learned more about how we are bringing the sacred into our secular lives. So, like a wandering pilgrim, I've been going door to door asking people where they find the sacred, and learning that each answer contributes to my knowledge.

I'm fascinated by the places on Earth that nurture and move us spiritually, both the well-known historical sites and the individually chosen places we go to for refuge and renewal. But more interesting to me are the stories behind the places, and the people behind the stories. At times, I've been allowed into the normally private depths of a personal drama as I learned why an individual cherishes a sacred place.

I think there is something unique about Cascadia, as the Pacific Northwest (including British Columbia, Washington and Oregon) is sometimes called, and listening to the experts gathered at the Cascadia Symposium at Simon Fraser University in the summer of 2006 convinced me that others feel the same way. We "secular but spiritual" Cascadians seem to be unusually averse to organized religion, as well as stubbornly independent and idealistic. We lean toward a belief in "nature religion," an Earth-centred spirituality that prompts us to sometimes lead the way in efforts to protect and cherish the environment. I sense a groundswell of spiritual searching, as many of us look beyond the traditional to satisfy our hunger.

The use of the word "sacred" and the phrase "sacred places" has evolved and expanded. No longer is sacred reserved mainly to describe religious buildings and what happens therein. Now, we recognize and speak regularly of First Nations sacred sites, which are part of land-claims issues in Canada and the US, and increasingly recognized as legitimate areas to be protected by legislation. Churches, religious buildings and monasteries are by definition sacred places, but now we include retreat and meditation centres, which may or may not have any formal religious affiliation, as well.

And going further, we have started to consider non-traditional locations as sacred, places we choose individually because of the way we relate to the spot or because of our history there. I'm thinking of the near-rapture on my friend Sharon Hall's face when she and I made the pilgrimage to Myra Falls in Strathcona Park on Vancouver Island, and she was able to immerse herself again in the roar and spray beside those waterfalls. This was the place where Sharon had first felt a sense of self-worth after fighting the demon of alcoholism. This was also the place that, once she learned she had terminal cancer, she wanted to return to before she died.

Most of us realize the intrinsic sacredness of a place of suffering, or of lost souls. Places of pain and death are often memorialized with a marker or, by families, with a roadside shrine at the place of an accident. These spots are imbued with the sacredness of the memory of loved ones. Skedans, on Haida Gwaii (the Queen Charlotte Islands), where hundreds of Haida people fell victim to the smallpox introduced by the white newcomers, is one of the most powerful places I have ever experienced.

I've been raking through the flotsam and jetsam of memory, trying to remember exactly when and why I became so interested in the concept of sacred places. I know Phil Cousineau's brilliant book *The Art of Pilgrimage: The Seeker's Guide to Making Travel Sacred*, was an early influence, as were Kathleen Norris's evocative writings in *Dakota: a Spiritual Geography* and *The Cloister Walk*. I've felt that many of the "yes" moments of my life were connected to a specific place, a place I make a point of returning to whenever I can, like the peak of Mount Albert Edward or the farthest campsite at Sombrio Beach. Gradually, I've become more aware of how much our approach and preparation beforehand—in other words, the intentionality we bring to a place—affects how we will experience it.

In British Columbia especially, the natural landscape is the reference point many of us use when we reflect on what is sacred. Even in the heart of our largest city, Vancouver, the natural surroundings are so stunning and present that I believe they are part of the psyche of all who live there.

Living on the Pacific Rim, a place betwixt east and west, between oceans and mountains, affects our view of the world in ways that intrigue me. I could probably happily spend the rest of my life investigating how we choose, cherish and create the places we deem sacred. And maybe I will.

Star Weiss
November 2007

I

Haida Gwaii: A Place of Spirit

Memories came out of this place to meet the Indians;
you saw remembering in their brightening eyes and heard it
in the quick hushed words they said to each other in Haida.

EMILY CARR, arriving at the site of the village of Skedans,
in *Klee Wyck*

-▸-◂-

I'VE NEVER seen a ghost, don't read Tarot cards and grew up in a clear-headed Protestant home where we took our religion straight up, without a drop of mysticism. So, when I climbed gingerly out of the floatplane, balanced momentarily on a pontoon, then jumped off onto the beach at Skedans, I had no expectations about what might happen next.

Just beyond the high-tide line, I pushed past bushes and young conifers, stepped onto the old village site and gasped. Several of the famous Haida totems still stood or leaned dangerously in their original locations. One memorial pole, tilting almost horizontally, was more than 40 feet long. Carvings of beavers, ravens, killer whales, bears and eagles were still identifiable, sometimes clearly visible, on the decaying mortuary posts and poles.

Nothing I had read prepared me for this sight or the way it affected me: the feeling started at my neck, flowed up and down my arms, back and legs, through my whole body. One cresting wave of sensation: goose bumps like I'd never felt

◄ Close-up of eagle mortuary totem, Skedans.

PHOTO BY JANET GIFFORD BROWN

before. This was my immediate, unexpectedly visceral reaction to Skedans, also known as Koona or K'una, on Haida Gwaii (the Queen Charlotte Islands).

-+->-<+-

H AIDA GWAII is an archipelago of islands placed like jewels off the north-western coast of British Columbia. It is in many ways perhaps the epitome of sacred places on the West Coast, a microcosm containing powerful elements that imbue this territory with its universally recognized mystique.

It has a richly woven First Nations history going back thousands of years; it is a land that has long embraced ritual and ceremony; it is a place where some people believe they can feel the presence of the Creator. Haida Gwaii is an isolated land of dangerous beauty: pristine, snow-capped mountains loom majestically above mossy, ancient forests and remote, wild beaches, and the constant presence of the sea envelops all.

It is a place apart from the ordinary, where the veil between worlds is thin, and the aura of the ancestors lingers. It is a legendary land where people listen for the language of Raven the Transformer. It's a place where spiritual geography affects daily life.

"There are places on this Earth that are spiritual, and on Haida Gwaii, there are so many places like this," Haida weaver April Churchill told me, as we chatted over tea in her living room shortly after my visit to Skedans. When I told her about my first reaction as I set foot on the village site, she was not at all surprised. She listened knowingly and then said simply that there is a "huge power in the ground" at Skedans and you "feel it through your body." April believes it's possible to "feel energy from the ground any place our people were working."

Even a month or two earlier, I could not have imagined that I'd be standing on the site of an abandoned Haida village on a chilly February day. But that was before I received an unexpected invitation from my friend Farah Nosh. Farah's passion—to bring world attention to the often-unrecorded daily suffering in Iraq and the Middle East, and see peace restored there—has drawn her back time after time to photograph the underbelly of war, the ongoing tragedy that destroys the lives of ordinary citizens.

Farah is also passionate about Haida Gwaii, where she has lived and worked in the past, and she knows these islands are a place of spiritual healing. She invited me to join her in a rustic seaside cabin on the Skidegate reserve. While Farah didn't exactly say it, I sensed from the start that there was more to this invitation than just a chance to be a tourist. I think she thought this would be a good place for me to mend my body and soul following several months of cancer treatment. After some hesitation on my part (Do I have the time and money? What about my job? Have I earned the "right" to an unplanned journey, a spontaneous trip?), I accepted her invitation and then allowed myself to become increasingly excited about the journey.

I flew into Sandspit, the tiny village where the airport is located, one grey February day, and, a few days later, my unlikely mid-winter trip to Skedans took place. Farah and her friend Janet Brown were both keen to join me, and I found a floatplane pilot willing to brave the trip at that time of year, provided we got a break in the weather. Fortuitously, just hours after a surprise snowstorm, the weather cleared and conditions looked good. Twenty well-narrated and scenic minutes after takeoff, we were skimming into a perfectly U-shaped bay where 27 dwellings once stood, and I was about to experience Skedans.

Now, only the rotting totem poles and traces of former houses mark the sacred ground used for centuries by hundreds of Haida families until smallpox, brought there by the white man, decimated the Native population in the mid-1800s. There is still a mournfulness at this spot. The presence of the ancestors is particularly strong at the old village sites, I was told later by Diane Brown. Diane, a well-respected medicine woman who has lived on Haida Gwaii all her life, believes the smallpox epidemics are partly responsible for the aura at these villages, saying, "When the epidemics hit, we weren't able to put people away properly. Their spirits still linger. Their presence is felt a lot."

⸸ ɩ ɩ ⸸

◀ Memorial pole on Skedans. PHOTO BY JANET GIFFORD BROWN

Perhaps the poignant heaviness cottoning the air around the totems was particularly noticeable because my two companions and I were the only human beings on the island and the first people to visit Skedans that year.

"There's nothing better than being first to a site," Diane agreed later, and something about the way she said it reminded me of being the first down a ski slope after a snowfall, a virginal exploration.

We took in as much as possible on our brief visit. Janet, who knew the island, led us to a huge, ancient alder tree near the village site. We were able to find remnants of the foundations of the village houses and nearly stumbled over reclining totems staring at the sky. We excitedly identified specific poles, using the book *Those Born at Koona*, by John and Carolyn Smyly, as our guide. We took photo after photo, hoping to capture our feelings on the images. I gently touched one totem for strength and stood for several minutes to marvel at the depth of the carved wings on another.

"I didn't anticipate how I was going to lose myself there," Farah said later. "You get there and it totally consumes you. All of a sudden, it was time to go and I wasn't ready to leave." Our visit felt unfinished, an introduction only, to the spirit of place on this spot. I was suddenly envious of Emily Carr, the iconic West Coast artist who was fascinated with the evocative beauty of the Haida carvings and who had the good fortune to spend a longer time at Skedans in the early 1900s.

"I went out to sketch the poles. They were in a long straggling row the entire length of the bay and pointed this way and that, but no matter how drunken their tilt, the Haida poles never lost their dignity. They looked sadder, perhaps, when they bowed forward and more stern when they tipped back. They were bleached to a pinkish silver colour and cracked by the sun, but nothing could make them mean or poor, because the Indians had put strong thought into them and had believed sincerely in what they were trying to express." [1]

I like to think of Emily sitting there nearly a hundred years earlier, sketching the same totems I saw, though by now, much of what she observed has been lost. Through her paintings, she introduced many non-Natives to the Haida culture at a time when few people knew much about it. Luckily for us, she arrived when the totems were much more intact, and she had an unusually foresighted appreciation of the significance of Haida culture and art.

Since her visit to Skedans, vines and bushes have overtaken many of the poles as they rot and return to the earth. It may be that in another 50 years or so, very little will remain of them. Some people wonder if more of an effort should be made to preserve the remaining totems. Or, since they often served as mortuaries and memorials, and are in effect Haida tombstones, should they be left untouched, as others fiercely argue, out of respect?

This is a question that also hangs over Ninstints, or SGaang Gwaii, the most famous of the abandoned Haida villages, with the largest collection of in situ totems in the world. (Skedans has the second-largest collection.) Ninstints, on Anthony Island off the southwest coast of Haida Gwaii, was declared a World Heritage Site by UNESCO in 1981. When I confided to Diane that I yearned to return to Haida Gwaii soon to go to Ninstints, I knew she understood by the way she sighed, "That's amazing there," and urged me to go.

Robert Bateman, the world-famous wildlife artist, conservationist and writer who makes his home on Salt Spring Island, BC, has travelled the globe to observe, paint and protect wildlife and their habitat, and considers Ninstints one of the most sacred places on Earth.

"I think there are four or five places I've been to that are really powerful and Ninstints is the only one in British Columbia," Robert said. (Other places on his list include St. Peter's Basilica in Rome, the sacred forest of Shinto-Ise in Japan and the Grand Canyon in Arizona.)

Yet Robert had two very different experiences at Ninstints. The first time he visited the site, it was a bright and sunny day.

"I don't think that's the right atmosphere," he told me. The harsh clarity of a blue sky seems to burn away the mystery of such a place. And the UNESCO crew at work on the island at the time, with chainsaws buzzing and people shouting, made the situation even worse.

Robert's account of his return to the same spot a day or so later evokes a completely different image, so vivid that even just listening to him, I could share in his sense of wonder.

On his second visit, Robert set out with just three others in a Zodiac inflatable boat. As he told it, the atmosphere was "mist. Still as glass. Pacific white-sided dolphins were jumping in front of the Zodiac, almost like spirits. Then a huge fin whale came up right beside the Zodiac, and we cut our motor. The whale rolled and looked at us with its eye, and sprayed. We sat there in stunned silence, all alone, in the glassy, grey ocean. Then we went to Ninstints."

After that magical interlude, Robert arrived, walked around the village site and realized that, in all his sacred places, "There's a human component ... I think the right kind of humanity really adds spirituality and feeling. It isn't just pure nature." His painting, "Spirits of the Forest—Totems and Hermit Thrush," inspired by the experience he had at Ninstints on his second visit, honours the ancestors by its evocative portrayal of wildlife and totems.

Diane honours the ancestors while accepting them as part of her everyday life. She is a Haida healer whose mother spoke to her only in Haida, telling stories and teaching Diane to use herbal medicines from the time she was a small child. Now, she does both herbal and spiritual healing. When Diane talks about the power spots on Haida Gwaii, her understated, down-to-earth manner makes what she says both believable and authentic. She always calls on the ancestors to come and help at the ceremonies she conducts, and recently Farah had the opportunity to feel their presence in a healing ceremony.

When Farah returned to Haida Gwaii after a photography assignment covering the 2006 war in Lebanon, she didn't realize she was suffering from post-traumatic stress disorder caused by the overwhelming effect that the tragic war images had had on her. When Diane saw Farah just after she had arrived back on

▼ "Spirits of the Forest—Totems and Hermit Thrush," painting by Robert Bateman, on his second visit to Ninstints. © ROBERT BATEMAN. REPRODUCTION RIGHTS COURTESY OF ROBERT M. BATEMAN, BOSHKUNG, INC.

◄ Diane Brown.

► Farah Nosh on beach at Haida Gwaii.

the islands, she feared what she saw in Farah's eyes and was worried about her friend. She invited Farah to take part in a healing ceremony at Balance Rock.

At first, Farah resisted Diane's invitation, not sure a ceremony was necessary, but late one night, sleepless and upset, she got up, drove to Diane's house and woke her up to ask her to go ahead.

Balance Rock is a huge, elliptical boulder left on the beach in the last ice age. The rock rests on a tiny portion of its stone base in a seemingly impossible balancing act and is a minor tourist attraction. It is also, according to Diane, a powerful place of healing. She frequently holds new- and full-moon ceremonies there, as well as women's healing ceremonies, and once took 45 Aboriginal healers from North and South America to the rock. She remembers clearly how moved the healers were by the power at the spot. Native elders and healers from all over the world come to Haida Gwaii and are always impressed by the number and strength of the power spots located throughout these islands.

Just before dawn, the morning after Farah's late-night visit to Diane's house, the two women headed to Balance Rock, built a fire and sipped hot coffee, while Diane made offerings of herbal medicines to the flames. The sun rose on a calm, windless morning, with the flames and smoke rising straight up to the sky. Diane prayed to the ancestors to come help ease Farah's heavy burden, and at that moment a gust of wind came over Farah's shoulder, a wind that gave her goose bumps. Afterwards, her heart felt lighter and she felt less stressed.

Farah hesitates in talking about this experience even now. "I wasn't expecting anything, because I didn't believe. I wasn't into that." But then she had the "amazing experience" on the beach and says she believes now that somehow she was being looked after by something beyond her understanding.

Diane said that a whole group of the ancestors came to help out that morning: she was aware of them. I've listened on several occasions to First Nations people talk about their relationships with the ancestors, a wisdom and knowing that goes

back for centuries. Despite my somewhat skeptical nature, I trust Diane's vision, and I'm thankful she and Farah welcomed the sun that morning.

I never expected to visit Haida Gwaii in 2005, but one thing I'm learning is to go where chance calls me and to be open to the element of surprise. The serendipitous leads us to the heart of our journey, a characteristic of any true pilgrimage.

2

What Is Sacred?

-+->-+->-<-+-<-+-

*What is significant about sacred places turns out not to be
the places themselves. Their power lies within their role in marshalling
our inner resources and binding us to our beliefs.*

THOMAS BENDER, in *The Power of Place*

-+->-<-+-

"I THINK EVERY place is sacred. I have many of them," Rabbi David Mivasair told me the first time I met him. "We create sacred space. My five-year-old daughter's bedside, my mother-in-law's kitchen, my garden, the holy blossom temple of a cherry tree."

I agree with David, yet I still don't have a precise, one-size-fits-all definition of sacred place. I'm not trying to avoid the question when people ask me, and I turn the question back to them. The answers are illuminating: the choice of sacred place is a kind of shorthand for recognizing what brings meaning into our lives, or helps us get through a crisis, the dark night of the soul, or gives us a sense of being connected to something greater.

Historically, the word "sacred" was rooted in religious experience. One dictionary definition is "dedicated or set apart for the service or worship of deity."

Most people can identify their sacred places without needing to nail down a definition. We are searching for a deeper level of meaning, both within and outside of organized religion, and we sense intuitively a place that feeds the soul and touches the heart. What threshold do we step across that elevates a location and makes a place feel sacred?

There are several commonly mentioned attributes of a sacred place: it is a place where we hope to transcend the ordinary, where we go to ask the big questions and listen for answers. It is often a place of solace and healing, or renewal and transformation, where we can be our most authentic selves. A place can become sacred through the force of memory: years of history on the spot and the power of repeated ritual seem to create an energy that is an echo of those who have gone before.

Some people would say a sacred site is a place where we are balanced between this world and the afterworld, with a foot in each, and can glimpse another reality. The phrase often used is "where the veil between worlds is thin." Many define a sacred place simply as a place where they feel closer to the divine or to God the Creator, either in nature or in a religious edifice.

Mircea Eliade, in his seminal book *The Sacred and the Profane*, says the sacred (the unreal or the pre-eminently real) is the opposite of the profane (the real) and involves an experience of the numinous (from the Latin *numen*, god) or the "wholly other"—a revelation of an aspect of divine power.[1]

People often say their sacred place is the place where they are in community in the deepest sense of relating to others. And sometimes the places we expect to be sacred don't end up feeling that way. As David the rabbi puts it, "A synagogue can be *not* functioning as a sacred space. Sometimes it's difficult to pray."

Places of pain, on the other hand, where grief is recognized, death is honoured and many souls are remembered, such as Verdun in France or Ground Zero in New York City, are often the most sacred of all.

Those who study geomancy, the art of reading the qualities of a place, or feng-shui may talk about sacred sites that occur at ley lines, energy or electrical currents under the earth—the Camino de Santiago is said to follow the ley lines of the Milky Way—or at a power point or vortex where specific energies align or are concentrated on the Earth's surface.

"Any part of the Earth is sacred by nature," including the ocean, beaches, mountains and deserts, says Heather Botting-O'Brien, the only university-appointed Wiccan chaplain anywhere in the world, as far as she knows, and an anthropology instructor at the University of Victoria. "Each [place] has a distinct spirit or energy of its own. I think some places definitely connect for various people.

"You can create a formal ritual space, a sacred space within a sacred space, anywhere, by drawing a circle," either by marking a line on the ground or simply pointing with your finger, Heather explains. "When the space is marked, that space is then protected and any energy that is raised in it is contained." The circle becomes the "holiest of holy" sacred places.

The phrase "sacred place" is applied differently today than it was a generation ago: it has moved along a continuum and is used to describe a variety of places. In recent years the words "sacred" and "spiritual" have, in a sense, been secularized, made accessible to all of us who are concerned about the future of the planet. We don't think twice about talking about the sacred Earth in normal conversation. With a bow to the Gaia hypothesis (James Lovelock's theory postulating that "all natural matter on earth, animate and inanimate, comprises a single, autonomous living being"[2]), the ecological movement and First Nations spirituality, we are rediscovering the sacred Earth. The relationship between faith and environmental issues is finally being seen as vital: mainline religious groups are now becoming actively involved in cherishing and protecting the Earth.

To me, the implications of this broader definition are fascinating and indicate a sea change in how we relate to the universe and embark on our individual spiritual journeys. In this time of transition to new norms, our expanded concept of sacred place is an opening that gives us another porthole from which to see the world. If we begin to see more places on the planet as sacred, we begin to develop a new appreciation of the preciousness of all parts of the world. For those of us who are not involved in a faith group, our recognition of a sacred place may be the way we feel spiritually connected to nature or to each other.

-→->-<-←-

T HE WORDS that cling to this topic are like chocolate truffles—they roll around on the tongue with a sense of mystery. "Sacred." Invoked in the mystical solemnity of a place of worship. "Sacred Earth." Affirmed in the passion of the environmental movement. "Sacred balance." David Suzuki's hope for the future of the planet. A whole ethos revolves around these terms.

"Sacred site." The rituals of thousands of years, a revered elder offering the gift of a song as a small group, accompanied by the rhythmic drummer, gather on the beach. "Sacred vow." "Solace." "Soulful." "Secret." "Sublime." "Sanctuary." (Is "S" a hallowed letter?)

"Sanctuary" is one of my favourites. I love the fact that it is both profoundly religious and thoroughly secular: it covers immense, impossible ground. Both saints and sinners are encompassed within it: St. Francis found sanctuary in a cave on an island in Italy; an escaped prisoner finds sanctuary in an embassy and cannot be touched. We create a nature sanctuary on the outskirts of a town, but it is really a reflection of that which is deepest within ourselves: a need to defend and care for the things we cherish most. Protection. Refuge.

Traditional and non-traditional sacred places can be categorized in various ways. I think of them as roughly falling into four categories: natural sites, First Nations sites, conventional religious sites and personal sites.

In the immense wild beauty of coastal BC, nature becomes our sanctuary, well, naturally. But it is in story and the repetition of story that we begin to understand and cherish the uniqueness of a place. It is personal, anecdotal history that elevates the singular experience of seeing a beautiful spot to a shared understanding of the sublime. For me Myra Falls, at the south end of Buttle Lake in Strathcona Park on northern Vancouver Island, has become a place of story. That story is about Sharon Hall.

-+->-<+-

S HARON HALL is one of those people who walked into my life in a fairly
ordinary fashion and whose distinct impact on my life was not expected. She
introduced me to sacred places that occur in nature, in spiritual retreat and in
facing death.

While she was a student in my journalism class, Sharon was diagnosed with
cancer, took treatment and hoped her illness was under control. But several
months later, the cancer returned: inoperable, terminal.

We became friends over those months of uncertainty, meeting for coffee or
lunch, keeping in touch. And then, partway through Sharon's treatment, I was
diagnosed with cancer myself. It seems ridiculous to add "to my surprise"—how
many of us expect to get cancer? But, as is so often the case when we face a
crisis, it does catch us off guard. It feels unfair, like a below-the-belt punch just
when we thought the round was going well. Now, unexpectedly, Sharon and I had
an additional bond, a connection punctuated by words like "chemo," "pathol-
ogy," "prognosis" and "goals."

During one of our far-ranging lunchtime chats in a noisy downtown restau-
rant, I asked Sharon if she had a sacred place. I've learned not to be surprised
when people can answer that question immediately, almost as if they've been
waiting for someone to ask. Without missing a beat, Sharon replied, "Myra Falls.
It's the place I want to go to again before I die."

We all tend to make flip comments like that, secure in the knowledge that we
have all the time in the world to carry out our plans. It's just a figure of speech.
In Sharon's case, however, she meant it. And as soon as she said it, I knew I
wanted to take her there. We planned the trip to coincide with good weather, we
hoped, and finally, one summer morning, we set out early, heading north on a
journey that we both recognized as a form of pilgrimage. The early-morning
start, the long, nine-hour round trip to the falls, seemed fitting: pilgrimage
requires that the experience be "earned"; reaching the goal needs to involve
making an effort.

▶ Sharon Hall arriving at Myra Falls.

I had a feeling that Sharon's reasons for being drawn to Myra Falls would make sense to me too. We were both fragilely full of anticipation that day: the feeling you hold inside when you're afraid that by brimming over, like a boiling pot, you'll tip the fine balance, make a mess of it. So, when we finally parked the car in the tiny parking lot near the falls and started our hike through the bush and trees, I walked behind Sharon with careful concentration, containing my thoughts.

"This is it, Star!" Sharon abruptly exclaimed, and there was that second of hesitation, the collective inhaling, that signified the importance of this moment to both of us. Then, she gently moved aside the leafy branches reaching across the path, like someone undraping a work of art, and stepped out onto the rocky ledge beside the falls.

As soon as we'd made our way carefully across the slick rocks, Sharon pulled out her camera and impressive 300-millimetre lens and started shooting the cascading waterfalls that tumble 70 metres down the cliffs into Buttle Lake. I watched her capture the falls with her lens, and knew I was witnessing a form of joyful communion. Sharon shot four rolls of film in the next couple of hours.

This was not a woman who was thinking of dying; this was a woman who was full-framed living. Despite what life had dealt her—a difficult childhood, a long battle with alcoholism and diabetes and, finally, a diagnosis of terminal cancer while still in her 40s—lots of good reasons to be bitter—she wasn't. Instead, she was a person who embraced the "cup half full" philosophy of life, a woman passionate about photography, lesbian rights, baseball and cats. She told me she was happier at that time than she had ever been. I realized later that one of the lessons she was teaching me was acceptance.

At Myra Falls, Sharon rediscovered an energy that gave her strength. "I can just feel it going through me. It's better than any drugs I ever took. A cleansing.

◄ Sharon Hall at the falls.

It's a feeling that stays with me, a feeling of peace. Time stands still." The constant roaring of the falls was "sweet music" to her ears.

Waterfalls seem to have that magical quality. When tourism, which began as a secular variation of pilgrimage, became popular in the 19th century, the number-one tourist destination in North America was Niagara Falls. Funny that today, spiritual travel, as the genre is becoming known, is once again hot. Sharon had had a "thing" for waterfalls for 30 years, ever since her family piled into a van for summer holidays in 1972 and visited places around the west. She drove her sisters crazy taking pictures of waterfalls wherever they went. And then, she was introduced to Myra Falls.

Our trip to Myra Falls years later was a "coming home" for Sharon, a home she never thought possible until 1994, shortly after she had finally faced, and worked to overcome, her addiction to alcohol. Friends from Alcoholics Anonymous brought Sharon, the city girl, to the wilds of Strathcona Park, and they stumbled upon Myra Falls, one of the best-known landmarks of the park, almost by accident. Thinking back to that transformative moment, Sharon remembered that this was "one of the first places that I realized I was okay, a human being. I had the right to be on this Earth. I belong here."

When she saw the falls, she felt as though God were talking to her, presenting her with this beauty. This was a shockingly new feeling for her. She calls it her "first spiritual awakening." The falls came to symbolize Sharon's rebirth, at age 37, into a world to which she finally felt entitled.

Her return to the falls with me was a time of mixed emotions for Sharon, and included an act of remembrance. She was mourning the loss of her friend Louise, who had been killed by a drunk driver exactly four years before. Louise's grandfather had had a trapline in Strathcona Park and loved taking his granddaughter with him on his rounds, probably not far from where we were standing. Louise had fought through alcoholism herself and was one of the watchful friends who helped Sharon find a way out.

Sometimes we face our fears by measuring ourselves against the elemental. Mountain climbers do so as a way of life. Sharon had found an elemental force, before which she felt both humbled and human, both consoled and in communion. At Myra Falls, she could remind herself that through all the hard times, "I never lost that sense of wonder, of adventure."

This spot on Earth was essential to her as a touchstone, but even when she was back in her city apartment, "I have it in here," she told me, pointing to her heart. She carried the feeling of power and peacefulness she felt at the falls within her.

The day after our trip to Myra Falls, I got an email from Sharon saying, "I'm a little sore after the hike, but emotionally and spiritually feeling just fantastic. It is a wonderful feeling reconnecting with myself."

Maybe this is the ultimate goal for any of us who seek out a sacred place: the ability to hold onto that feeling of peace or energy or renewal, that sense of *place*, even when we're not actually there.

3

Bumping into St. Clare's Monastery

-+->-+->-<-+-<-+-

I do not have to go
To Sacred Places
In far-off lands.
The ground I stand on
Is holy.

MARY DE LA VALETTE, in
Life Prayers from Around the World

-+->-<-+-

I DIDN'T EVEN know I was on a pilgrimage until I was already well along the path and committed to going farther. When I think back though, maybe part of me did know. When I wandered into the church at Cape Mudge on Quadra Island and realized I was listening to a gifted poet muse on life, as Native elders served freshly caught salmon, homemade bread and wine for communion, maybe I knew. And when I unexpectedly found myself on the grounds of a monastery in the forests of Vancouver Island, meeting contemplative nuns and when, against all odds, these women became part of my life, I did know something must be going on.

It may seem logical, even predictable, that at least one monastery would be included in this book on sacred places. St. Clare's Monastery is, after all, a place that deeply touches a variety of people. But I never would have foreseen the profound effect this monastery and this group of people have had on my life, or even that I would ever have a reason to go there. I'm not Catholic, and I'm not

◄ The hermitage at St. Clare's Monastery.

▶ St. Clare's Monastery, Duncan, BC.

sure I even knew monasteries for nuns existed in my part of the world, despite my fondness (yes, I admit it) for *The Sound of Music*.

But I'm learning that sacred places are like good friends, each unique, each meeting our needs a bit differently, each filling a distinct role in our lives. Certain places, like certain friends, centre or ground me.

St. Clare's Monastery has become one of those places, and I fulfilled a long-held desire when I took time out to stay for a few days in a tiny hermitage on the monastery grounds. This cosy little one-room hut is available for guests to occupy from time to time and is a place for quiet moments, for walks in the woods and for listening, if you choose, to the daily prayers and singing during chapel services. I spent four slow days there, taking time out to clear my thoughts and become closer to the rhythms of my heart.

But let me back up a bit, to the first time I drove up the shady driveway to St. Clare's Monastery, hidden away in the forest off a quiet road in Duncan, BC. I was a little nervous, curious and expectant. I had never been to a monastery, nor had I met any of the Sisters of St. Clare, also known as the Poor Clares, who awaited me. My relationship with the sisters and their monastery at that point was purely professional and very much by chance. An editor at the Victoria *Times Colonist* newspaper had given my name to the Poor Clares when they called the paper, looking for coverage of their upcoming celebrations to mark the 800th anniversary of the birth of St. Clare. Sister Joyce Harris dutifully called me and asked if I would be interested in writing up the services they planned.

This was a first for me. But, while I knew nothing about monasteries, I was immediately intrigued by the thought of learning more about the lives of cloistered nuns in the late 20th century. When we bump into unexpected situations, they sometimes set off a chain of surprising events: our circumscribed world is

shaken, not stirred. I wonder sometimes if there is indeed a grand design influencing our lives, even leading us to our sacred places. Looking back now, I realize that this experience was part of my journey, as necessary as watering a plant that is in danger of drying out.

I approached the monastery, a rambling, single-storey, cedar building with an adjoining chapel, and rang the doorbell. I introduced myself and was warmly welcomed by Sister Joyce, the nun who had contacted me originally. She led me to the sisters' large and airy parlour, where I sat with a group of about 10 nuns in their circle of welcome and immediately felt at ease in their midst. They, in turn, appeared genuinely glad to meet me. The sisters, who ranged in age from about 45 to the venerable nonagenarian, Sister Louise, seemed comfortable with who they were and remarkably clear about their purpose.

As Sister Barbara put it, "We believe that in opening ourselves to God, we help humanity. We carry the world's pain in prayer. We're all connected, so, when anyone is able to open themselves to a greater reality of love, it reaches everyone."

Such certainty about life's path is unusual these days, in our fractured, busy lives, and I envied the sisters their clarity. From my vantage point years later, I realize that what I found most alluring was, and is, the distinct community they have created: people live, work, pray, laugh, sing, play and die together. Their relationship to each other is a constant, with a level of trust and intimacy not often found, even in a biological family. Their relationship to God is one of constancy as well, with a commitment and single-mindedness that provides direction, focus and a daily connection to the divine.

The sisters have formed a community that is ever changing, yet immutable; that is always busy, yet has found a stillness; that is enclosed, yet embraces the outer world; that is deeply spiritual, yet very ordinary, replete with the mundane tasks of daily life. Within that community, facing many of the same challenges we all face, they have created a space where good things take place, where people care about each other and pray for peace and for solutions to the problems that confront us, where strangers are welcomed with warmth and grace, and where the beauty of the Earth is celebrated every day: a sacred place.

"We all know there are places of evil on the Earth," Sister Dawn Marie said to me once. "Why not create a place of goodness?" Why not indeed? Maybe that's one way we can work toward balance in our long-suffering world.

I wondered how other people feel about the sacred ground of this monastery, and the sisters suggested I talk to Maarten Schaddelee, an internationally renowned sculptor, and his wife, storyteller Nadina Schaddelee. The story of the sisters is interwoven with that of Maarten and Nadina. Even Maarten's close brush with death, as he lay motionless during a heart attack, seems to have been an inevitable part of the saga that brought him onto stage left with the sisters. He and Nadina are part of their drama, as surely as "Get thee to a nunnery" was uttered by Hamlet in Act 3.

Prior to his career as an artist, Maarten had worked in the family business for years, helping to run the Dutch Bakery in Victoria. His life changed after he suffered his near-fatal heart attack and decided to "follow his bliss," as Joseph Campbell put it, and try a new vocation as a marble sculptor. Not just any marble: Maarten wanted to sculpt Carrara marble, the same Italian marble Michelangelo chose, and he began looking for a local source of Carrara. Nadina was more than a little skeptical, but to their surprise, Maarten soon located three pieces of "used" Carrara marble, formerly the base of a statue of St. Francis, at Stewart Monumental Works Limited, right in Victoria.

The marble slab, it turned out, had belonged to the Sisters of St. Clare, who left it behind when they moved from Victoria to their new monastery in Duncan in 1973. The heavy pieces were awkward and the people at Stewart's were anxious to get rid of them. The first time Nadina touched that marble, she said, she could feel the energy within it, and soon the marble was lugged to Maarten's seaside workshop adjacent to his home.

Maarten and Nadina, suddenly the new owners of this beautiful marble, wanted to know more about it. Finding out the story meant phoning its former owners, the Sisters of St. Clare, who invited Maarten and Nadina to talk about it over tea.

"Tea" at the monastery is both a ritual and a festive event, with most or all of the sisters in attendance. One sister greets visitors at the front door and ushers them into the bright and spacious guest parlour, with chairs and couches arranged in a loose circle. The other sisters enter from the hallway, dressed in plain brown jumpers, white blouses and sandals. Tea and coffee are prepared in a small kitchen off the parlour, and goodies of various types are served on small china plates. Everyone is introduced and then, invariably, a stimulating chat begins, punctuated by warm laughter. The visitor or visitors are the focal point, and thanks to the sisters' listening skills and genuine interest, any visitor is made to feel that he or she is the most fascinating person the group has ever met.

Looking back on that first occasion and the many that have followed, Maarten said, "At that point, our lives changed, and we met these most wonderful, wonderful women. I think of them as an extension of my mother. When we're sitting in that circle, it almost makes me weep."

When I asked Maarten and Nadina, both raised as Protestants, to try to describe to me why they felt so drawn to the monastery, they said, almost in unison, that it was the sisters themselves who made it sacred. The sisters have created a spiritual aura and hallowed ground, by virtue of their presence and intention on that spot.

"They [the sisters] could be standing downtown and make it sacred," Maarten said. "For me, wherever they stand is sacred. It's just a feeling, when I'm with them."

Nadina expressed a similar feeling. "Not only spaces are sacred, but when that intention of grace is happening, then that which is created in that space is sacred … They [the sisters] are reflecting to you the gift of who you are."

Is this perhaps what we're seeking in sacred spaces? A place of grace, where we can find the authentic "I" in each of us?

Eventually, Maarten created two sculptures that he gave to the sisters, one of the hand of St. Francis and the other a bust of St. Clare. The bust was originally intended for his own personal collection, but, after lugging it back and forth to the monastery for several events or occasions, he and Nadina realized that the piece belonged on the monastery grounds. St. Clare is perched gracefully at the front of the monastery, a "greeter" for those who visit this sacred place.

→>-<←

Anne Nguyen came to Canada when she was two years old, in 1980, as a boat person, one of the thousands of people who fled Vietnam and found a new home in Canada. Years later, after finishing her undergraduate degree, she went on a retreat with the university's Catholic Student Association, and first heard about the Poor Clares from a student who described them as "joyful women who dance."

When a bookstore salesclerk later told Anne that the Poor Clares also had a tiny hermitage on the monastery grounds, which outsiders can stay in, she was immediately interested. At the time, she was working hard for a non-governmental

◄ The Sisters of St. Clare in their parlour.

organization in Victoria and was just back from an intense trip to Vietnam. She called the sisters and asked to stay in the hermitage for two nights.

"I felt like I'd come home," Anne said. Raised a Catholic, she found herself drawn to the prayer hours in the monastery chapel and "felt my heart open when I was there." So she kept going back, every month or two, for as long as she was in Victoria. "The Clares are some of my favourite people in the world."

The location of the hermitage, set apart from the monastery on a small rise in the trees, is a particularly sacred spot for Anne. "The monastic way of life is attending to very small things," she said. In her quiet times there, she looked at the trees, the spiderwebs and the dew, and spent time gathering leaves to press or walking slowly around the grounds.

She said, "I do feel like their space [the monastery] is very special and their land is very special, but I feel that way about all of Vancouver Island. I think that all of Creation is sacred, but we're not in the frame of mind to see that, but there [at the monastery], the people *are* in the frame of mind to appreciate that."

The natural and domesticated beauty that people take time to appreciate on the four hectares that make up the monastery grounds includes the local giants, hemlocks, cedar and Douglas fir, along with arbutus, alder, maple, dogwood and flowering bushes like lilacs and native rhododendron. Shooting stars, chocolate lilies, camas, bluebells, yellow and purple violets, buttercups and trillium bloom every spring and summer. Woodpeckers, owls, deer, raccoons and otters share the property. Nuns in blue jeans kneel in the soil to tend the large vegetable garden behind the monastery, and the flower garden in the inner courtyard includes spring bulbs, roses, clematis, camellia and lavender.

The sisters' favourite circular walk takes them through the back property, where two more small hermitages, used only by the nuns, are hidden among the trees.

One of these, the Clare Hermitage, with electricity and running water, is surrounded by tall evergreens and wildflowers, and is, appropriately enough, Sister Clare's favourite sacred place "for times of refreshment, solitude and prayer."

The monastery chapel is one of Sister Joyce's favourite locations, which she described as "a place of spiritual nourishment for me, partly because of the

Blessed Sacrament, and years and years of praying people create an atmosphere. It looks out on creation, and takes in the inner and outer." Sister Joyce's background includes a Ph.D. in counselling and clinical psychology. When I asked her for her definition of sacred place, her answer was characteristically complex and thoughtful. "For me, one of the truest sacred spaces is within the person … From my perspective, everything is sacred," a viewpoint that is also held by many First Nations in North America, and one that mainstream religions are belatedly beginning to embrace once more.

"But," she continued, "there are spaces that help you to drink of the mystery that is God … places that have held the mystery of human experience in some way and people continue to come for calmness, peace, a weaving of inner place and outer place that makes it sacred.

"Sacred means heightened, intensified ambience, the air is electric, a creative energy, but it's in stillness too. It brings us into that depth of stillness and quiet within our being and people are hungry for that … We need these places that help create the opportunity for us: when we go there, we're putting ourselves in the setting."

As I listened, I found myself thinking again of the importance of balance in our lives: the yin and yang; the active and the contemplative; the electricity and the stillness. Maybe so many of us feel overwhelmed in our daily routines simply because we are out of balance.

In the voluntary simplicity of the monastery, I can stop and focus and feel something almost magical: a sense of being unconditionally accepted and acceptable, and held firmly in the prayers of a group of people who, if there were a praying Olympics, would be in the running for a gold medal. The monastery has become a touchstone for me, a place I need to keep going back to, to know that I'm on track.

Within the societal microcosm the sisters have built, they have found a way to create joyfulness, to "make a joyful noise," that is a paradigm for others. The comfort of being within an intentional community, in a peaceful, natural setting, in the company of witty, deeply religious women, generates a sacred energy.

4

Walking the Labyrinth

-+->-+>-<+-<+-

In a maze we lose ourselves, in a labyrinth we find ourselves ...
Our spiritual quest, I feel, can be summarized as this single
obligation: to switch from life-as-maze to life-as-labyrinth.

Robert Ferre, *Living in the Labyrinth*
by JILL KIMBERLY HARTWELL GEOFFRION

-+->-<+-

I MAY YET become a believer in labyrinths after the experience I had on the beach at Tower Point, in Witty's Lagoon Regional Park, Metchosin, BC, one summer morning. My companion, Joanne Thomson, urged me to walk to the centre of the huge labyrinth she had just drawn in the sand, reminding me that if I went in with a question, I would come out with an answer.

Here's the problem and also a truth-telling moment: I felt awkward, as though I were play-acting somehow, when I walked a labyrinth as if I knew what I was doing. Ever since I started on this personal pilgrimage, I keep coming across labyrinths, and I've tried hard to overcome a mixture of skepticism and New Age–related embarrassment about them. As my odyssey continued, I have found, a bit to my surprise in fact, that my viewpoint is changing.

The term "labyrinth" is used in current parlance to describe a path that follows a circuitous but clear, unicursal (single) route to the centre. A "maze," by contrast, is a complicated puzzle, which includes myriad, confusing paths and

◄ Joanne Thomson and her beach labyrinth.

dead ends. I've talked to earnest, thoughtful people about this ancient tool. I've walked a brick labyrinth beside a church and met with the former prisoner who laid every brick. I've wandered through the portable canvas labyrinth laid down in an interfaith chapel. I even tried walking a planted, 11-circuit labyrinth, with a border of small shrubs, but that labyrinth found me out.

Here's what happened. The day I walked the garden labyrinth at Meg Hansen's seaside home in Saltair, near Chemainus, BC, I was in a hurry and thinking about a ferry I had to catch. I had spent a leisurely afternoon drinking tea and interviewing Meg, a trained labyrinth facilitator. Although we both knew this was a rushed time for me and not really fair to the process, I asked to go walk the labyrinth, taking photos along the way. I barely had time to get to my ferry, hence the urgency.

I was not sure of my role at that moment: was I a labyrinth walker or a writer/photographer at work? I walked quickly along the path that wound into the labyrinth, thinking I was on my way to the centre. Suddenly, I was on my way out again, just a few feet from the exit, having managed to get off course and completely miss the meditative heart of the labyrinth. Meg and I laughed, bemused, and I was aware that I was being taught something valuable. Since I was too hurried to enter into the labyrinth experience with my full concentration, the labyrinth was not "letting" me get to its essence. I was denied entry. I thought about this as I drove off, time-limited and humbled just a bit. Maybe there was more to this labyrinth thing than I had originally thought.

The power of place and ritual is not always what we expect it to be. As I researched and wrote this book, and met so many people who have been comforted, transformed, rejuvenated by their sacred places, I began to think that there is something happening here that doesn't fit into our everyday vocabulary. It sometimes feels like points of light on a map that could become one glowing globe, a sphere or planet of sacredness, once we get it right: the sacred Earth.

At Tower Point, Joanne set about creating her labyrinth. She likes the world writ large and on the beach she has a vast, sand canvas. We were barefoot, the early-morning sun warming our feet. The snow-frosted Olympic Mountains

◄ The labyrinth at Saltair.

loomed in the distance, and the sense of space and light was so acute it felt to me like we were standing in an amphitheatre in the centre of the universe. In fact, the ancients in various cultures believed their sacred places *were* the centre of the world, (the Greeks called it the *omphalous*, or navel), from which all else emanated.

I watched Joanne walk in larger and larger circles, dragging a hefty stick behind her like a plough, cutting a deep, satisfying groove in the wet sand. She completed her huge, ephemeral design and walked the labyrinth, slowly and meditatively. Then she invited me to do so, and, in this almost surreal and magical moment, within a natural setting of simplicity and beauty, I started my walk. I tried to ignore my nagging sense of doubt, to just relax and give in, to "be in the moment."

I walked into the centre with no clear question, but I was aware of the recent loss of a dear family friend, a prodigious author who was universally described as "kind," and much beloved by children, especially his own two grandchildren. I mourned his loss to this world and then the thought came to me: "You are needed as a grandparent."

I did not have any grandchildren but was ever hopeful. Two and a half months later, my daughter Holly and son-in-law Dean told us that their first child was on the way; they were barely three months into the pregnancy. Coincidence? Probably …

But I could never have known then how *much* I would be needed immediately after the birth. I was present for that wondrous event, and still there when the new family faced a medical crisis that meant they needed extra help caring for their little daughter. I stayed on to help out for the next several weeks. Because I was needed. Because I was part of the circle of love that is family. As the family made its way through those difficult days, I remembered the thought that had come to me in the labyrinth. And it did make me pause.

▼ Star walks the labyrinth.

-+->-<-+-

T HE SAND labyrinths Joanne creates on the beach are places of transformation, she said, designed to be transitory, to open a threshold briefly, so she can step through into "a journey to the unconscious."

Historically, the labyrinth was designed to mimic the path of the soul, and that appeals to Joanne, who wants to recognize both the light and the dark—joy and happiness, pain and anger—in her life.

"We spend a lot of time trying to ignore the negative in life, and it's still there," she said. "If we can accept the negative, it loses some of its power."

After her father's death, Joanne turned to the labyrinth as a safe and private place to face her grief. "I went into the centre and I wept and allowed myself to grieve, for the things he never got to do, for the things we never talked about. I needed to grieve the man I didn't know. On the way out, I looked at how I could use my father's life for lessons of my own. He was a painter. He talked about colour and infinity. So I've looked at that too, and incorporated them in my work."

When you walk the labyrinth, Joanne said, "You enter the non-speaking world, quiet and timeless. It's a place we move in and out of, secure in the knowledge that the way in is also the way out. "The labyrinth is the whole metaphor for existence. That's what a sacred place is, isn't it?"

My introduction to the modern use of labyrinths came from Henri Lock, United Church chaplain at the Interfaith Chapel at the University of Victoria. I remember being surprised when he first mentioned labyrinths, somehow thinking of them as vaguely pagan (which they were, way back, but

they have now been a Christian symbol for centuries. Looking back, I'm a bit embarrassed at my ignorance, but I've heard others say the same thing, so here's a chance to set things straight).

Henri told me about the portable labyrinth created by UVic students to help them deal with the stress of exam time each December and April. I'd never thought of labyrinths as stress relievers, but I was intrigued and decided to go see the student-made canvas labyrinth when it was placed on the floor of the chapel one April.

Just before the labyrinth is rolled out each semester, Henri normally gives a labyrinth workshop and talks about the labyrinth as a symbol of our spiritual journey. He encourages people to "walk into the depths to be transformed and then out to our lives."

Maybe that's why the labyrinth design has become popular in recent years. We find ourselves drawn to unconventional forms of spiritual practice: tools that help us forge ahead on a different, but intuitively attractive, path. The labyrinth appeals to this search for an alternative place of meaning, and is proof as well of the importance of ritual, even in a time when we are rejecting more traditional forms. So I stopped a while and walked the labyrinth on the chapel floor, a good example of the adaptability of this ancient design. It was a quiet, contemplative walk, and the skepticism and silliness I'd felt seemed less evident.

The labyrinth is a walking meditation, a pseudo pilgrimage. In medieval times, would-be pilgrims who could not make the trip to Jerusalem would go to Chartres Cathedral in France, considered one of the most sacred Christian sites, and walk the labyrinth built into the floor there, as a substitute for the actual journey. This practice was deemed an acceptable show of true faith, and the Chartres labyrinth was walked so often for this purpose that it became known as the "Chemin de Jerusalem," or Road of Jerusalem.

Meg Hansen considers her labyrinth a sacred place, a horticultural-therapy tool and a place of healing. Aryana Rayne sees exciting possibilities for the future: she and her group, the Victoria Community Labyrinth Society, dream of building what they believe is the world's first equal-access labyrinth.

Aryana is the coordinator of the society, whose proposal is for a unique labyrinth to be built on a site yet to be determined in downtown Victoria. The Victoria Community Labyrinth Society is a group of primarily blind and visually impaired people who have enthusiastically joined with Aryana (who is sighted) on her personal crusade to build a labyrinth that can be used by anyone, handicapped or not. The model has artistically designed railings, smooth brick pathways and extra room in the centre and at switchbacks for easy wheelchair manoeuvrability.

Aryana took one of her visually impaired friends to the labyrinth outside Victoria General Hospital one day. She held a scarf behind her and her friend grabbed the opposite end. Afterwards, Aryana's friend glowed as she talked about what it felt like to walk without assistance, a rare experience for her. That's the kind of experience Aryana and her group would like others to have as well.

A wooden finger labyrinth, about a metre across, leaned against a wall of Aryana's office, and she said a man first crafted one of these for his autistic grand-child to use as a calming device while he is in school. When the child is agitated, he simply lets his fingers do the walking on the desktop labyrinth, and it helps to balance and soothe him.

Aryana discovered how much she enjoyed walking the labyrinth at St. Paul's Anglican Church in Vancouver, Canada's oldest permanent indoor labyrinth, and loves the way labyrinths "bring in movement." Now, her passion is to develop "tools that people can use themselves, so they can heal," and she believes the equal-access labyrinth could make that tool available to everyone.

-+->-<+-

WHEN RICK WOOLDRIDGE told me about the project he had been part of, I realized that labyrinth building can lead to community building as well. Rick's story is of an unusual collaboration that I first heard about from Michael Hadley, co-founder of the Restorative Justice Coalition at William Head Insti-tution. Michael was actively involved in the unusual joint effort by parishioners

and prisoners to build a labyrinth in the churchyard of Christ Church Cathedral in Victoria as a millennium project. He suggested I interview Rick, the brick-layer for the project, and a good person to tell me all about it

Rick and I met on a bench beside the Christ Church labyrinth one cold, blus-tery morning. He was wearing sweat pants and a zip-up jacket, and greeted me with a broad, slow smile. He was an inmate at William Head Institution, involved with the Restorative Justice Coalition, when he became involved in the labyrinth project in 1999. In his opinion, it was a perfect example of restorative justice in action—a chance for those who had erred to begin to make amends by working on a project in which members of the community welcomed their assistance.

When the work-release inmates first met with the church group on the prison grounds, "Everyone clicked immediately," Rick said. As the practicalities of building the labyrinth were discussed, he quietly told the group, "I know how to put down paving stones." His grandfather had been a bricklayer in Holland, and had always hoped his grandson would follow his trade. Here was the perfect chance.

The day the labyrinth was built, participants dug a 38-centimetre-deep hole in the churchyard; then sand, stones and crushed rock were shovelled in, raked and levelled. Next, Rick laid each brick by hand, holding the top and gently drop-ping it into place, about 8 centimetres deep. The bricks were tamped in, by foot and with a tamper.

"I'm the kind of guy, I get on something, I'm do do do until it's done. I'm a workaholic and addictive personality, I guess you could say," Rick laughed.

Starting from the centre of the labyrinth, Rick and the group worked slowly outward. Time after time, the centre brick was lifted out to allow the workers to

◀ Rick Wooldridge and "his" labyrinth.

meticulously adjust and tighten the labyrinth. They dumped sand and more sand from wheelbarrows, tamped the sand, laid the bricks, levelled, tamped and adjusted bricks carefully when they started to sink. Rick went through three pairs of steel-toed work boots and four pairs of gloves as he dropped and banged each brick into place. The work was all completed in one 24-hour period. Under the centre stone are the names of all those who worked on the labyrinth, along with a millennium loonie.

While Rick was talking to me, reliving that day, two young teenagers wandered into the churchyard in front of us and walked the labyrinth. We both watched them silently, then Rick turned to me with a smile. "I feel rewarded, thanked, every time I see someone walk my labyrinth."

"The prisoners put a part of their souls into this project," Michael told me later. As the project unfolded, he watched the changes in parishioners' perceptions when they worked side by side with the men from the work-release program. "The process itself was a transformative experience."

Michael added an epilogue. One inmate who worked on the project died shortly after it was completed. To honour his memory, Michael met at the labyrinth with a group that included the man's six-year-old daughter. Leading the little girl to the centre of the labyrinth, Michael placed her hand on the bricks and told her that her father would always be there. Like any place commemorating those we've lost, the labyrinth is now a place of remembrance as well.

The brick labyrinth in the cathedral churchyard broke down barriers and helped people really see each other, sometimes for the first time. A labyrinth is a tool that increases our awareness through movement *and* contemplation.

5

Cascadia Tales: The Wanderer's Path to the Sacred

—✦>–✦>–◄✦–◄✦–

You can travel many miles, but if your heart hasn't changed, you haven't gone anywhere.

Anthony, Anglican priest on a desert pilgrimage,
in *The Role of the Guide in the Practice of Pilgrimage*
by MURRAY GROOM

—✦>–◄✦–

ALKING WITH Sister Maureen Wild under broad-leafed maple trees at Glenairley Centre for Earth and Spirit in Sooke, BC, one sunny autumn day, I asked her why she thought so many people seemed to be turning to nature to fulfill their spiritual needs. Maureen, a Sister of Charity, studied ecological ethics at St. Michael's College at the University of Toronto and has spent time and energy looking at the relationship between ecology and spirituality.

"Formal religion wasn't nourishing and something else is. We're all born as spiritual beings, I believe, and when people make the choice to leave doctrine, they have time to allow their own spirituality to grow in other ways."

Maureen's comment seemed to support my own observations of people being on an alternative search for the sacred, which, to me, is what we're doing every time we consciously identify and think about our sacred places.

In fact, this province is notable for its secularism, atheism and just plain lack-of-church-going-ism. Let's take another look at the oft-quoted statistics on our religious affiliations, or lack thereof. In the 2001 census, 16 per cent of Canadians nationwide said they have "no religion," a statistic that has been steadily rising. In BC, the percentage of people answering "no religion" (the "religious nones" or even just "nones," as they are called) was more than double that, at 35 per cent. In 1991, 30.4 per cent of British Columbians and 11.3 per cent of Canadians overall answered "none." Whereas in 1901, 1.5 per cent in BC, versus 0.2 per cent in Canada, answered "none."[1]

And yet, while the percentage of "nones" is definitely rising, and only about 40 per cent of the BC population are active participants in institutionalized religion,[2] another trend seems to be emerging at the same time, according to Statistics Canada.

The Statistics Canada Summer 2006 report, *Canadian Social Trends*, confirms that public religious affiliation and attendance are declining in Canada (and especially in BC) but goes on to say that half of adult Canadians "regularly engage in religious activities on their own."[3] These activities include prayer, meditation, worship and reading of sacred texts. The report didn't include an activity called "going to my sacred place," but it did say they "engage in such private religious behaviour either at home *or in other locations*." I wouldn't be surprised if some of those locations were the places people have identified as their sacred places. (At least, it seems logical and probable that this could be the case.) And of course, home can often be a sacred place as well.

Professor Lynne Marks, a historian at the University of Victoria, has studied the history of secularism in BC and believes that "in many ways, British Columbia was born secular." She explained that BC's low number of church-goers per capita is not a new phenomenon but dates back to the late 19th century. She attributes this historical trend to the fact that, when immigrants started arriving in numbers in BC, they were a transient, primarily male workforce, far from the religious roots of family and influenced by labour radicalism. There was a common late-19th-century saying that men left their religion behind them when they crossed the Rocky Mountains.[4]

In the last 30 years, however, since the publication of Rachel Carson's *Silent Spring* and the growth of the environmental movement, Lynne has observed a paradigm shift. She agrees that people are rediscovering the idea that the Earth is sacred and becoming more aware of the places that are most worthy of protection.

Tina Block, who teaches Canadian and BC history at Thompson Rivers University, has studied religious and secular beliefs and trends of the '50s, '60s and '70s in BC. She has found that many British Columbians consider themselves spiritual, but think that going for a hike and communing with nature or serving their communities and being kind to each other is more meaningful than sitting in church pews. "Mountains and sea were understood to be at least partially responsible for secularizing the quintessential Northwest lifestyle."[5]

Tina found when she interviewed British Columbians about their "irreligious behaviour" (that is, their lack of regular church attendance), the reasons they gave to explain it included the fact that, since BC is "an outdoorsy kind of place," they would prefer to take a Sunday drive to the mountains to enjoy nature, rather than sit in church. People said they lived in the Garden of Eden, or that the climate was so good that they'd simply rather be outside.[6]

Along with the natural-splendour argument, Tina believes that BC has somehow established a reputation, and even an expectation, of being an "unchurchy" place.[7] In her opinion, "while the region has been, and remains, a place of abundant spiritual energies, over time irreligion has become entwined in the myths and expectations of Northwest culture."[8] People don't perceive the Pacific Northwest as a conventionally religious area.

Douglas Todd, spirituality and ethics reporter for the *Vancouver Sun*, is always interested in the question of how we in the Pacific Northwest, particularly in BC, are pursuing our spiritual quests and religious beliefs. While at Simon Fraser University as a fellow, Doug assembled a group of scholars and others well versed in the subject, and hosted a symposium, Cascadia: Spirituality, Geography and Social Change, in August 2006. Doug often writes and talks about the effect our spectacular landscape has on our psyche and our spiritual

◀ Sandy pocket beach at Welbury Point, Salt Spring Island.

lives, and how we turn to nature, a walk in the woods or a hike in the mountains, to feel close to God, or to deal with stress.

I asked Doug where his sacred place is, and his answer was twofold and illuminating. "Sometimes I walk through the trails of Pacific Spirit Park, next to the UBC campus. At times, I've found the beauty of it—especially the myriad shades of green—so strong that it's actually been disorienting. I feel gratitude for the solitude and the infinitely complex wonders of creation."

Then Doug, who was raised in a "strongly atheist family" (an interesting credential for a religion writer), mentioned another place as well. "Despite the stereotypical arguments against it, I often feel a sense of the sacred in buildings that are part of institutional religions. That feeling of awe and centredness comes in part from enjoying designs that are devoted to something other than money and success and pride. But it definitely also comes from being among a community that's honest about our fragility and that's devoted to being open to moments of tenderness."

In a talk Doug gave on sacred spaces, he amplified his feelings. "In 2006, when it's trendy to think of formal religious edifices as 'empty' of the spirit, I have to admit the first time I actually entered a church, which was at age 19, was also when I first realized what people meant when they talked about the sacred. It didn't hurt that the first church I ever entered was England's Salisbury Cathedral. It took my breath away. The sheer architectural magnificence, the soaring pillars, evoked a sense of transcendence, of awe, of the ineffable presence of a reality beyond the ordinary. It may have been the first time in my life I really realized how people could be religious."[9]

Two thoughtful choices of place, one natural, one architectural.

As Doug points out, we in BC are prone to contradictions when it comes to our spiritual lives. Despite our low rates of participation in organized religion, we still identify as people with spiritual needs, who more often than not say that we believe there is a God. At the symposium, Doug wanted to look at trends in all of Cascadia—that is, British Columbia, Washington and Oregon—a region with shared dramatic topography and, it turns out, similar trends when it comes to religion.

Gail Wells, an Oregon-based, natural-resource writer and editor interested in religion and spirituality, and a speaker at the symposium, started out by saying there is so much public land in Cascadia that it has shaped the art and literature of the area, which is "very rooted in place. People from New York had culture and we had scenery."

I sat up when she said that. Okay, I'm from New York (many a long year ago) and I think I get what she's driving at. Is that one reason why I'm on this quest? Am I still trying to figure out the significance of all this—*scenery?* If I had been born here, would I be as enthralled with its beauty? Is natural splendour a counterbalance to culture (and religion), which can generate an elemental, even spiritual relationship with our surroundings so that we don't need the mediating layers of formal religion? Is culture, on the other hand, just one big effort to find another path to the divine?

Gail says, in fact, that the "nature-based spirituality" she sees in Oregon relies on an experience of the divine; that is, people find awe and wonder in the natural world that enriches and gives meaning to their lives. Nature is considered sacred. The ideology of nature-based spirituality is behind the fight to protect old-growth forest, since the trees are sacred and worthy of protection in their own right.[10]

Patricia O'Connell Killen, professor of religion at Pacific Lutheran University in Tacoma, Washington, said at the symposium that in the post-modern age we live in, we Cascadians don't organize ourselves in institutions the way we have done in the Modern Age (roughly, the 18th to the 21st centuries). Instead, we tend to go it alone and associate in "looser, more networked groups of limited duration." Individualism is highly valued throughout Cascadia. In Oregon and Washington, as in BC, organized religion is "fragile"; the numbers of people inside religious institutions are a minority (in the mid–30 per cent range for Oregon and Washington).

The overarching narrative for our area, according to Patricia, is "the West" itself, a place where humans encounter grandeur in the landscape and there is no one prevailing religious group alongside which to define ourselves. In a region

▶ Myriad of greens in Pacific Spirit Park.

PHOTO BY PILLE BUNNELL

where the geography is "so immense it swallows you," Patricia mentioned that places for pilgrimage, for example, mountains or First Nations sites, are significant.[11]

The phrase "secular but spiritual" was introduced by Mark Shibley, a sociologist at Southern Oregon University. He came up with the term to describe those who are not affiliated with an organized faith group, but who are exploring spirituality and spiritual issues in their lives (typically, those who say, "I'm not religious, but I'm a spiritual person"). Mark, who has studied spirituality and religious life in the Pacific Northwest for years, says there are many people who feel this way.

He goes a step further and thinks a significant number of Cascadians are participants in what he calls "nature religion," an Earth-based spirituality that is influenced by the indigenous tradition, the secular environmental movement and Pacific Northwest literature. Authors like Barry Lopez and Gary Snyder espouse this.

Mark uses the word "religion" advisedly, but for him, the fact that believers in Earth-based spirituality develop rituals, share a world view that reveres nature, and become part of a communal effort in an organized group, like the environmental movement, proves his point: this is more than just a personal moment of ecstasy in nature. He goes so far as to call nature religion "the soul of Northwest culture," and thinks that many, if not most, people here experience the sacred in nature.

In Mark's view, the region is not so much "less religious" as it is "differently religious ... The search for meaning, transcendence, and belonging continues in unconventional ways. The sacred abounds."[12] I guess that's partly why I'm on this quest: I want to find out where that sacred is abounding. But, after hearing these astute, well-researched observations from people who spend their lives studying the social trends of Cascadia, a few things seem clear. The wilderness environment around us affects us (we find God or the divine in the grandeur); we

realize we are eclectic, multicultural and Eastern facing (hence, faiths like Buddhism, Hinduism and Sikhism each have an effect on us); and we recognize we have a history of attracting Utopian dreamers and life-on-the-edgers who are drawn to our frontier-tinged Pacific lifestyle. Increasingly as well, we non-Natives are learning to appreciate the spiritual beliefs of our First Peoples and the sacredness of all things. So, where do we go to find our spirituality?

Douglas Todd chose both a forest and a religious building as his sacred places. He may be on to something that reflects an underlying human need that has revealed itself to me more clearly as I researched this book.

One "Aha!" moment for me was my descent to the depths of Shawnigan Creek with Murray Groom, minister of Sylvan United Church in Mill Bay, BC. Murray and I met one November day at the trailhead, which is at the top of a long wooden staircase that follows the creek to its mouth far below. There are close to 100 slippery stairs and as we clambered down them, Murray talked about how, for ages, the religious have been "taming the wild" by trying to convince people that wildness was not part of religion. Now, he believes that "the Earth-oriented spirit is coming on" again.

"There is a groundswell of people saying there is more than just the taming," Murray told me, adding that people are recognizing and reconciling the dualism of what he calls "the priest and the shaman" or "the temple and the tent." The

◄ Murray Groom at Shawnigan Creek.

priest in the temple represents the comfort and security of the traditional religious home base, for example, a church, whereas the shaman in the tent represents the freedom of someone on pilgrimage, searching in the wild. That wilderness search may take people to places they don't expect, exposing them to risk and surprise.

On that late fall day, as we climbed downward, Murray and I were the pilgrims, walking (that's significant: Murray think it's important to feel your feet on the ground) to a sacred place. Maybe the slimy stairs were part of the risk. We descended into greenness and roaring, a primeval scene that brought us closer to the heart of Mother Earth. We paused beside the lush rainforest gully just above an inlet of Mill Bay. The thundering below us was the sound of the falls at the very bottom of Shawnigan Creek, the energetic last push of the rushing water before it emptied into the bay. Coho salmon migrate here each fall, fighting their way up from the ocean, assisted by fish ladders. Murray likes to come here then, when the river runs high.

Above us was the Island Highway, with cars whizzing past, their occupants unaware of the hidden beauty underneath them. It seemed an apt metaphor for the subconscious depths running beneath our daily thoughts, waiting to be discovered if we stop and take the time.

For Murray, taking the time means intentionally creating opportunities in his life when he can get a "glimpse of another reality, a reminder of the wild. Revisiting his sacred place at the mouth of the creek is one way to get that glimpse.

"It needs to be a place set apart," he said. A sacred place—barely perceptible—where we stand on the threshold, creates a tension as we move through and then come back, and this moving back and forth, this intermittent-ness, preserves the spot's specialness and holiness. "If it's common, it loses its frisson, its cachet. It needs to be visited occasionally. You have to move away from it to really appreciate it."

Historically, Murray says, a pilgrimage is a return to where we came from, a return home to our origins, which offers the possibility of an encounter with the holy or the divine. The pilgrim arrives at a sacred place, which Murray defines as an intersection between Heaven and Earth. This transitional place can take many forms: that day, it was the spot where the fresh water of the creek mingled with the salt water of the sea.

Murray's church is located a few kilometres up this same creek, right beside the water, and the symbolism of this is not lost on him. On Halloween (a day of transformation) in 2004, the congregation met on the far side of the creek, dressed as saints or sinners—a lot of angels and clones of St. Francis, Murray remembered—and proceeded to make a pilgrimage across the bridge, like crossing over Jordan, to their new church, built to accommodate a growing congregation. In many traditions, water is a symbol of purification, and in Christian and Jewish tradition, crossing water is a significant act, a holy crossing. Walking to the sanctuary was, as Murray put it, a transition from the wandering, churchless "tent" period to the security and solidity of a new "temple."

The new church, Sylvan United (the original town near this site was known as Sylvania, because of the surrounding forest) is another of Murray's sacred places, one that appeals to his need to be grounded in a church congregation amidst tradition, continuity and community. Later, he took me there as well. A children's choir was practising—the songs floating out to us—as we lingered and listened.

Murray believes we all have an innate sense of the sacred and are now finding ways to fulfill our longing for it, to take part in our own pilgrimages and return to our sanctuaries. He showed me two of his sacred places that day: one of the shaman and one of the priest, the two types of guides. Both, he believes, are a part of our search for the sacred in our lives.

Murray gave a vocabulary and authority to unnamed thoughts and vaguely guilt-ridden concerns that had been on my mind for a long time and legitimized my alternative search for the sacred. Whether through wandering or pilgrimage, I've been a nomadic and eclectic seeker, moving my "tent" from place to place as I continue my quest. When Murray admitted he too is a searcher and welcomes the mystic within that makes him want to leave ritual and go wander, it somehow validated my own erratic ramblings to find the sacred in unexpected places.

6

The Songs Stay There Forever: First Nations Sacred Sites

→>-→>-<←-<←

New stories are sung from contemplation of the land.
Stories are handed down from spirit men of the past who have
deposited the riches at various places, the sacred places.

Pat Dodson in *Sacred Sites, Sacred Places,*
edited by DAVID L. CARMICHAEL, ET AL.

→>-<←

IT'S IMPOSSIBLE to think about sacred places on the BC coast without being ever aware of the history here, going back thousands of years, of the First Nations communities and their relationship to the land. Even with the best of intentions, however, I doubt that any non-Native person can fully appreciate the sacred pact between the natural world and the Aboriginal peoples who have lived here for so long.

"The land is sacred because it's been here for thousands and thousands of years, and people have been dying on this land for thousands of years, right here, where I'm sitting," said Tsartlip Elder Tom Sampson, sitting in the living room of his home on the Tsartlip reserve in Central Saanich.

Tom is considered an authority on the cultural significance of sacred sites of the Saanich people; when I arrived at his home for our interview, his papers were spread out on a long table and he told me that the chief had just left. He had also come to talk to Tom about the currently hot issue of sacred sites. As a respected

◄ Tom Sampson.

elder, environmentalist, former Tsartlip chief and chairman of the South Island Tribal Council for more than 20 years, Tom is someone whose voice is listened to carefully. He knows the stories, struggles and heritage of his people, and has been working virtually his whole life to honour the traditions of his ancestors and improve the lives of First Nations people. His advice to the chief was to get instruction from the spirit world by making offerings of food to the ancestors and waiting to hear what they say to do next.

Tom has thought, written and spoken about sacred sites for most of his life: he was an eloquent speaker defending the sacred mountain YAAS during the controversial proposal for a new town at Bamberton in the 1990s. In 2006, he was one of the elders whose wisdom was sought during the controversy that swirled around the protection of a sacred cave on a section of the upscale Bear Mountain Resort property in Greater Victoria.

His answers to questions about sacred sites aren't cut and dried, or crisp, like a bureaucratic memo. Instead, they are organic, flowing, even poetic, describing a personal journey, a process rather than a result. Maybe that's one reason we can't seem to get our heads around the concept. World views are at variance here; even the idea of property "ownership" differs. Two cultural paradigms co-exist uneasily, and that means we have to be willing to really listen. That skill, as Tom well knows, is increasingly rare, no matter what the culture. I'm hoping that, in the quiet of Tom's home, on the spot where his family has lived for generations, it will be a good place to hear what is said.

I asked Tom what makes a place sacred and he told me it's about a person experiencing something, a person offering him- or herself to the Great Spirit, with careful preparation beforehand. He said there are two stages to this process. The first stage is QE,ĆASET, a SENĆOŦEN word which means to prepare yourself for a journey never before taken, a vision quest. The journey begins when a person gets to the point in life when he or she wants to know about the trees and the mountains, to understand all of creation. The journey begins with prayers to the spirit world for protection.

"When you go to a place to pray, you don't want others to intrude, don't want to be disturbed. You go without water or food or life's pleasures, you deny yourself so you are absolutely pure and clean when you come in the presence of the Creator."

The preparations for communicating with the Creator include fasting, ritual bathing at daylight and offerings of prayers and song. These rituals bring to mind the elaborate preparations for pilgrimages prescribed by many religious traditions around the world, both past and present.

The next part of the process is known as STENOLECET [1] and means to journey or travel to seek a new understanding and way of life. This can happen at puberty or when someone becomes a dancer in the longhouse or when they are ready for their vision quest. As a person embarks on this journey, he or she finds and helps to create a sacred place. This place becomes a personal place of spirituality, a place to cleanse him- or herself, find better understanding and receive visions of things that could be.

"It becomes that person's sacred ground and they must protect it," Tom explained. "A person goes there to be in the presence of the Creator. You find your humanness there. Not everyone will find it, or use it."

Ceremonies, such as mask dancing, are then used to protect the ground, and once that is done, the ground is protected for all time, Tom said. "You can't 'un-sanctify' it."

Specific songs also become associated with, and remain at, the spot. Tom told me the story of one local politician who came to ask about the drums and songs he kept hearing from his home, even though he could not find anyone there.

"The songs stay there forever, because the Creator says this is the song that will stay there," Tom told the man, not at all surprised that the sacred songs could still be heard. "When you give a song a purpose, then it becomes real."

The ceremonial place for the song may be a cave, a mountain, the sea, a lake, a river, a spot where people go "to seek advice and discipline. In this journey and walk, we come to understand life and we find out and learn about the sacred place, a place to go to communicate with the Creator."

▶ Terry Point at the place of his ancestors, Garry Point.

The places mentioned by Tom are universal. Cultures around the world have recognized the sacredness of the towering mountains (which reach upwards to the heavens, often considered home of the gods or God), of grottos or caves (places of retreat and initiation), of bodies of water (which cleanse and purify us) and of groves of trees (a symbol of immortality honoured throughout the ages by cultures around the world).

Tom thinks we need to take time to try to find out what's going on around us. "We don't take time out, but the trees talk to us long before the wind comes. The widow tree will tell you there's a storm coming. You can't learn from books, you have to go out and write your own experience."

Archaeologists have made many mistakes, Tom believes, when they assume that just because they can't see something, it's not there. "They have to take time out to ask 'Why is it I can't see it?' We're so arrogant about our role in the world … Our world is in a crisis, not just war, but the environment. The trees are dying. The flavour of the land guides the fish and men back to the sacred fishing grounds, but now that's being destroyed by oil and chemicals." Those left behind will pay the price, Tom said, because our environment is being burned and sacred places destroyed.

"People have lost their inner spirit. They're just a shell … They took spirituality out of the schools … This is not about religion. This is direct communication with the Creator. I don't need a priest or shaman to tell me. We don't need middlemen."

However, Tom believes that "tragedy always rekindles hope," and he does have hope. The homeland of his people has become "the sacred mother," and to protect her we must learn to "hear with [our] eyes" and "see the song."

-+>-<+-

MORE OFTEN than not, it is First Nations elders I have spoken to about the importance of sacred sites, so it is a particular pleasure to hear about work being done by the younger generation. Terry Point is a 30-year-old Musqueam

man who has spoken publicly about the significance of sacred places, and, as a First Nations student in the Langara College Aboriginal Studies Program, was actively involved in mounting the Site to Sight: Imaging the Sacred exhibit at the Museum of Anthropology at UBC in 2004.

When I learned that Terry had given a talk at the Richmond Museum about how humans define sacred places, both man-made and natural, during Heritage of Faith Week in 2005, and had been interviewed on CBC Radio on the subject, I was excited and intrigued. He was someone who had obviously given a lot of thought to the subject of sacred places, and he took the time to meet with me and show me his personal sacred place one fine spring day.

We met at Garry Point (*qw'uya'khw*) Park, a flat, open piece of land jutting out to the sea, perfect for kite flying or family picnics, and once the home of Terry's ancestors. This sense of history is vital to Terry, who told me, in his soft-spoken, likeable manner, "I think you need a sacred space because the world goes too fast, moves so quickly. A place to reflect on what we're here for, to get a grip ... For us First Nations, we have a relationship to the land, a teaching, for thousands of years. Others don't have that, aren't tied to the land, can just get up and leave. But for the First Nations, there's a sense of responsibility and thinking seven generations ahead."

The idea that we should make land-use decisions that we believe will stand up to the test of time, seven generations' worth, is an oft-quoted First Nations concept, which I can only hope the decision-makers are listening to more carefully today than ever. As Terry said, the fact that people haven't been making far-sighted decisions "is the main reason for the problems."

Terry sat gazing quietly out to sea on the rocks at the far end of Garry Point. His family's village was right here for thousands of years. Terry got his family name because his ancestor, Munėlh, who lived and fished at Garry Point, sold fish to a French buyer who could not pronounce Munelh's name. Instead, the Frenchman called him "Charlie Le Pointe" or Charlie from the Point, later shortened to Charlie Point. In the 1950s, when the government threatened to take away their Indian status if they did not move to the reserve, the villagers left the site and moved to Musqueam Reserve #2.

From the time he was 12 years old, Terry worked every summer on the fish boats off the point on the South Arm of the Fraser River. Looking out over the Fraser now, he can feel the ancestors, who fished there for hundreds of years, watching him. That's hard to imagine for someone like me: even in my own lifetime I have moved from the east coast to the west, changed countries, rolled like a tumbleweed.

When I asked Terry how the rest of us wanderers can feel connected to the land, he told me, by "creating sacred space." The question is: how do we go about doing that? Maybe we can start by working together, learning from each other.

"In order for us to progress as First Nations, we need to solidify relationships with all sorts of non–First Nations communities and build awareness of our culture here," Terry said.

One way he did that was on by working on the Site to Sight: Imaging the Sacred exhibit. The exhibit grew out of an anthropology assignment.

"We started by exploring what each member of the class thought was 'sacred': we came up with everything from personally created sacred places such as a bathroom designed to relax you during a bath, to patterns that occur naturally in nature and ones made by humans such as graveyards. I even discussed how I as a football fan made a trip to Oakland, California, to watch a football game and tried to explain how it was like a pilgrimage to watch our heroes play a game." Our ways of seeing the sacred depend on our cultural knowledge and on our expectations, Terry said, and Site to Sight tried to explore this idea. As the exhibit information stated, "Ongoing traditions of sacredness have existed for thousands of years throughout Vancouver."

-+->-<-+-

"WHEN I THINK of being Musqueam and sacred, there are many things that are considered sacred and are not shared," Terry said in his speech at the Richmond Museum, citing, as an example, the secret sacred society *sqwayqway*, to which you must belong in order to be entitled to dance specific mask dances.

The Musqueam people have a phrase, "*tu sniw kwthu syuwenulh tst*," which translates as "the teachings of the ancestors handed to us" that encapsulate all things: both living things and inanimate objects such as rocks and trees' as well as mythical beings like the Thunderbird.[2] Because of these teachings, people know to honour the ancestors with a memorial celebration four years after their death. The most sacred building for the Musqueam people is the big house, or longhouse, where traditional ceremonies and spirit dances take place. Those ceremonies are also protected, kept secret, as they are in many First Nations cultures.

-+->-<-+-

THE SACRED relationship between humans and the land that Tom and Terry spoke of is based on ancient teachings—taking time out to listen to the trees and to the elders is an essential part of wisdom.

7

A Different Kind of Sacred

→>-+>-<+-<+-

*Because of the Unitarian emphasis upon the questioning mind
and upon the unrestricted use of reason, our church should not
give an enclosed and darkened impression but should rather
convey an impression of light, air, and space.*

PHILIP HEWETT, Minister, Unitarian Church of Vancouver,
in written instructions to the architect

→>-<+-

WE HUMANS are pretty good at creating sacred space architecturally, stone by stone, brick by brick, and have been doing so for thousands of years. Temples, shrines, cathedrals and a plethora of places of worship around the world are tributes to our desire to honour the gods or the Creator.

But I was curious about a church building that straddles the fine line between sacred and secular, trying to be spiritual without being overtly sacred. In fact, members of this church are, according to Executive Director Mary Bennett, often uncomfortable even using the word "sacred" (though she thinks that may be changing). "God" is probably not used much either.

It is the Unitarian Church of Vancouver, a destination that was included without equivocation in the Vancouver Heritage Foundation's 2004 Sacred Sites Tour. The church may be difficult to categorize for some people, but to others it is an example of a site that balances the sacred and profane in a humanistic, dualistic creation that recognizes the complexities of the secular-but-spiritual life of the West Coast.

The resulting complex, completed in 1964, was the first post-1940s building added to Vancouver's City Heritage Register. The covered arcades connecting the buildings, the cubic composition, the large central courtyard and gardens, and the lofty, airy church itself were designed to be "a kind of revolt against"[1] traditional church architecture, just as the Unitarian Church itself represents a departure from mainstream Christianity.

"In this revolt against the traditional church, it was important that the buildings and the grounds would not only serve well in the practices of the Unitarian Church, but should also become a symbol of a different view of the world," wrote the church's architect, Wolfgang Gerson, in 1991.[2]

Long-time Unitarian Church of Vancouver member and lay chaplain Karl Perrin has been attending Sunday services at the church with his family for more than 20 years. Karl grew up Unitarian in the United States, joined the Peace Corps and went to Afghanistan. He was a conscientious objector and an active member of Students for a Democratic Society, left-wing activists of the 1960s, and to him, the Unitarian Church is, among other things, a "nursery for activists' groups."

Karl remembers the scent of lilies and the feeling of lightness when he first entered the sanctuary of the Vancouver church, a place he calls "magical." He found himself returning, partly for the superb classical music. Wolfgang, the church architect, was a talented musician, as well, and used to play the piano and occasionally the harpsichord.

"I come to get rejuvenated, to put aside what's going on in the world, to recharge, and connect with the community here, to go somewhere deeper," Karl said. He has also found his niche as chair of the church's environmental committee. "I work toward this [church] being the centre of my universe." Funny to hear his choice of words: that's how ancient cultures like the Greeks thought of their sacred places, too.

The Unitarian Church of Vancouver is a place for being in community, Karl said, "sacred without the sanctity," with no apologies: a building to house and

▶ The sanctuary of the Unitarian Church of Vancouver.

allow inspiration. And since the floor-to-ceiling windows and skylights unite the indoors with the trees and sky so successfully, "You are almost outdoors when you're in this church."

That, according to Wolfgang's daughter Kate Gerson, a third-generation architect (whose sister Erika is also an architect), is completely by design. "The space is very connected to the earth." The glass wall panels and huge windows surrounding the sanctuary create a transparency, a looking-out at nature. Even the materials used in the construction, richly hued woods and concrete, provide a modernist feel of warmth and openness.

Wolfgang Gerson grew up Jewish in Hamburg, was forced to leave and eventually wound up in Canada, where he became an active Unitarian. It's not surprising that he tried to avoid any sense of hierarchy and to establish an egalitarian feel in this sanctuary. Back in the tumultuous 1960s, when Wolfgang was designing the church, he wrestled with basic questions of the future of religious buildings in his notes and letters: "Was a modern church a place of not very specific functions, and civic uses which could change over the years, flexible spaces? Or should it indicate stability as we are also all yearning for some form of stability in the turmoil of contemporary ideas?"[3]

His answer was to try to incorporate both needs. The sanctuary or sacristy was "the quiet stable element changing only slowly and allowing for the repetition of ceremony,"[4] and the fellowship hall and religious education building (now known as the Hewett Centre) allowed "adaptable spaces inside."[5] "We have both a longing for permanence and for change,"[6] Wolfgang wrote.

Wolfgang lamented the "extraordinarily featureless" site of the church, in a dramatically situated city of "ocean, mountains, and lush growth"[7] and worked with this drawback by placing the church on the highest and quietest spot on the property.

"It is open to the sky, as it is open to the trees and the nature of which we are part ... It is also the Temple of Light, or if you wish, enlightenment of the Magic Flute. Some of you know of my great admiration for Mozart and the Magic Flute, and its temple created this image in my mind immediately."[8]

Constructed as a cube defined with equal sides, the church has a relationship to nature that is also realized through the choice of materials and the play of light that illuminates the space, even on a dull day.

"Man must be seen as an integral part of nature, rather than a special creature dominating nature,"[9] Wolfgang maintained. "In all my designs, the open spaces and enclosed spaces are of equal importance."[10]

The overall design concept is based on Unitarian principles given to Wolfgang by the minister at the time, A. Philip Hewett, who wrote, "There is no universal agreement among Unitarians, as there is in most denominations, concerning what they are doing or trying to do in church." Hewett admitted that the real reason for the "vast Gothic edifices" erected by and for Unitarians in England and America in the 19th century was to "convey to the community at large that they were just as important a religious body as any other [and] had the resources to put up just as imposing a building, ... and that they would do it."

Hewett then hastily added, "None of us would want to put up a building that was simply boastful ... but there might be some acceptable means whereby the building could speak of Unitarianism to the community ... The principles to be expressed in this way, if possible, would be inclusiveness rather than exclusiveness, breadth of view as against narrow-mindedness or reliance upon one tradition alone, and a forward-looking spirit rather than one tied to the ideas and

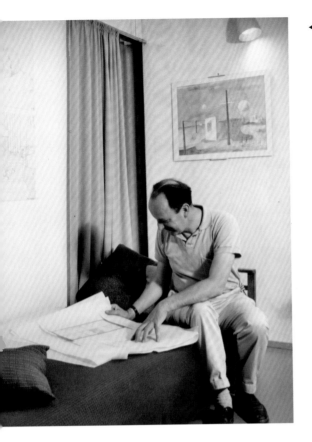

◀ Architect Wolfgang Gerson.
PHOTO BY SELWYN PULLAN

practices of the past."[11] Other important elements were "a basic simplicity that combines beauty with functionalism, a gathered-around-feeling of fellowship," and an emphasis on life and growth.[12]

Wolfgang's job was to transfer Hewett's ideas into architectural reality. Intention (to reflect Unitarian principles) informed design (the architecture of the church), which in turn resulted in a physical expression of values in what he himself referred to as a "non-church church."[13]

A minor controversy discussed in Wolfgang's letters and reports points out his dry sense of humour and personal resolve. He was objecting to the proposal to apply a dark stain to maintain the exterior wood of the church building and wrote, "The proposed dark brown would produce a restless vulgar jumble ... we should try to retain the idea of expressing the natural colour of the material, which we felt to be an idea appropriate to Unitarianism. Otherwise, I would suggest that each member of the congregation take the paint pot with his favourite colour to the building and paint his bit of trim in the most democratic shared contribution to the church. My favourites are rose blush and mock purple combined."[14]

This skirmish fought with artistic fancy is reminiscent of the film *Rainbow War*, a hit at the 1986 Expo in Vancouver, and brings to mind an image of a multi-hued church welcoming the masses, with Wolfgang, arms folded, smiling on the sidelines.

Speaking of decor, Wolfgang felt strongly about the addition of the hand-sewn tapestries depicting two flames that hang at the front of the church, and defended them eloquently at a service, saying, "Buildings are containers which never seem completed without accretions of people and their objects."[15] ... "Seeds in the flames are being opened up by the fire; symbolizing (if you want to) the continuity of life and death, a British Columbia version of the Phoenix. They ... will shock some that are used to the very quiet atmosphere of the church now."[16]

The Unitarian Church of Vancouver was Wolfgang's "most substantial and recognized building," Kate said: it received an award for excellence of design in 1965, the judges commenting that the church gave them "a warm and compassionate" feeling. "The fact that he [Wolfgang] could 'live in it' was very special to him." Kate was even married in the church, partly because her father "bribed her with music."

Kate believes her father succeeded in creating a "non-threatening religious space"; weddings, funerals and "infant namings" are often held there for people with no religious affiliation. There are no crosses in the building, no doctrine that must be followed, and you don't have to talk about God. Growing up in Vancouver, Kate said, grinning, she had no vocabulary of "spirituality" or "sacred," and her mother wasn't wild about the term "church" as the building was being constructed. The full name, Vancouver Unitarian Church and Centre, came later.

Kate said that when she was a teenager, the church was the centre of social life for her and Erika, where they learned about "sex, drugs and rock and roll" in a liberal, accepting, yet safe environment. For Kate and her family, this space was "very much a place of comfort ... In North America, one's neighbourhood is often not as important; this [church] community *is* our neighbourhood."

From an architectural point of view, said Kate, the design stands up well even now, despite the fact the church is built in a way "we couldn't get away with today, because the envelope between the inside and outside, with glass and one slab of uninsulated concrete, is so thin." The upside of that is a "much more successful indoor-outdoor relationship." The complex where the church sits includes the courtyard, a meeting centre with a large hall and classrooms, an administrative building and a large garden.

The church has a wonderful lightness and seems to exemplify the all-encompassing spirituality that is often characteristic of life on the West Coast. I listened to Karl and Kate reflect on what it is like to be a member here, in this church that is not exactly a church, in a congregation that prizes intellectual inquiry, social activism and inclusiveness, where the goal is to search for meaning while making ethical decisions that respect all people *and* the environment, and I realized this is in many ways a distinctively British Columbian model. On this coast, where the concept of "sacred" is bubbling up from the stew of our eclecticism, it seems that Wolfgang Gerson was somewhat prophetic in his vision of a sacred place as an open space of welcome and philosophical discourse.

8

Mountains

➤-➤-➤-⋖-⋖-⋖

LA'U WEL<u>NEW</u> is our sacred mountain and through the use of
this mountain all the spirit symbols will help our people find a new
clear vision for the Saanich people and pass it on to
all our children through our education system.

The late PHILIP PAUL at the opening ceremonies of
LA'U WEL<u>NEW</u> Tribal School in Central Saanich, BC

➤-➤-⋖-⋖

IKING UP a mountain is an alpine pilgrimage: it involves effort and
planning; it is a journey that dwarfs and humbles us; it is an encounter
with the unknown. Standing on a mountaintop is a spiritual experience
that remains mysterious for me.

From ancient times, humans have recognized the sacredness of significant
natural forms around us—mountains, trees, caves, water—and intuitively sensed
the link to the divine in nature. In traditional societies, a mountain was seen as a
connection or cosmic axis between sky and earth, and I think it is hard to stand
on a mountaintop, anywhere, and not feel closer to the infinite, the Creator, the
unanswerable.

Sacred mountains have been identified and revered throughout history, and
I've been lucky enough to stand on the tops of a few of them, from Mount
Olympus in Greece (where I placed a tiny stone in memory of my friend Pam,
who I feel sure helped give me the courage to reach the summit) to Yasur

◄ Our hiking party on the way up Mount Albert Edward. (*Left to right*, Dean and Holly Broadland, Russ and Star) PHOTO BY DEAN BROADLAND

Volcano in Vanuatu (where the gods must have been angry, because we were chased off by a sudden terrifying eruption of red-hot lava rocks around us).

My family has hiked up mountains from the time our young daughters were strong enough to do so, and this ritual is one of the most satisfying spiritual traditions in my life. But the mountain that is a part of my family's collective consciousness through memory and ritual is Mount Albert Edward, located on Forbidden Plateau (a sacred territory itself) in Strathcona Provincial Park on central Vancouver Island. One day it became clear to me that this mountain is hallowed to others as well.

We'd been hiking for several hours along the ridge that leads to the summit, and just as our group, consisting of Russ, our daughter Holly, our son-in-law Dean and me, reached the final slog to the peak, we heard a helicopter approaching. We were in the high reaches of the park, and the only helicopters we'd ever seen in the area were bringing in trail supplies or taking out waste near a campground far below us. A small group of people had gathered, waiting for the helicopter to land on a flat area just before the scree slope.

We stopped to watch and asked what was going on, as helicopters are not normally permitted to unload passengers within a provincial park. We were told that the passengers were the parents of a well-loved Boy Scout, a teenager who had died tragically. They had managed to get permission to fly in and walk the last bit of trail to scatter their son's ashes from the peak of Mount Albert Edward. I think the mother had broken her ankle and couldn't hike in herself, hence this special dispensation.

Watching the assembled mourners—Scouts, leaders and family members—slowly hike upwards, I thought about those parents and how the spirituality of mountains is a force that affects so many of us. The group headed quietly to the summit, a 2,000-metre perfectly pyramidal peak that looks like a child's drawing of a mountaintop. We gave them their space, but we couldn't help but be affected just by being in close proximity to a ceremony of remembrance carried out on a spot that feels like the top of the world.

Mount Albert Edward (which our daughter Kristi called "Mount Live Forever," when she was little) is the second-highest peak on Vancouver Island, and once you are on top, you can turn completely around and see nothing above you but sky. You can walk right to the far edge, and look down, down, from a dizzying height into an open chasm. I can almost feel my stomach lift as I think about it now. Over the years, that place has become part of my psyche, and long ago Russ told me that, if possible, he'd like his ashes scattered from that peak too. "How will I climb it when I'm 93?" I quipped, but I know how he feels.

Mount Albert Edward was the first mountain Holly and Kristi ever climbed, and our stories there began that day. On that hike, we met and motivated a group of young offenders "sentenced" to a tough Outward Bound hiking expedition. Our young daughters started to out-hike the teenage boys but, "No little kid's gonna pass me!" one of the boys grumbled, as he picked up his pace and hurried by us. I have no doubt that the repetition of ritual and accumulation of family lore we've amassed while climbing that mountain year after year is part of its magic for us.

I remember coming down from the mountaintop late one summer's day, our long shadows leading us across the rocky plateau, watching my daughters skipping and laughing ahead and hearing Russ just behind me, and knowing this was my church, halfway to heaven, a place I feel God's presence. And realizing that I was glad to be in this place with my family.

My relationship to mountains is limited to the last 30 years or so, but I know that for our First Nations, the sacredness of mountains has been understood for thousands of years. To hear the First Nations perspective on mountains, I turned to two respected members of the Saanich Nation who each have an intimate knowledge of their sacred mountains, and who pass on teachings that go back centuries. And who are worried about the future. The two mountains they believe survived the big flood and provided refuge and protection for the Coast Salish people are YAAS and LA'U WELṈEW̱.

➤➤◄◄

WHEN JOHN ELLIOTT talks about LA'U WELNEW, he speaks quietly, with time for reflection and pauses that emphasize his carefully chosen words. He is not in a rush: the people of the Saanich Nation have held this mountain sacred for 10,000 years, and John, a SENĆOŦEN language teacher and historian, knows he is simply one voice in a long narrative. But there is a steely determination in his voice just the same, as he calmly tells me about what LA'U WELNEW (also known at Mount Newton), on the Saanich Peninsula, means to him and his people.

From the time he was very young, John knew that LA'U WELNEW, or the "place of refuge," was the most sacred mountain of his territory, home of the thunder people, and the spot where, it is said, his people tied up their canoes 10,000 years ago to escape the big flood. He grew up knowing the story: when the storm was over and the flood receded, the people untied the rope from an arbutus tree and promised not to burn its wood (a promise some keep even today), and declared the mountain a place of refuge. At that time, said John, "It became our sacred place; it became our church."

From that day to this, he says, the Saanich people have used the mountain as a place for prayer, fasting, meditating and other rituals. It's the place where young warriors carry out vision quests, where initiation rites are held and where people go to feel connected to the Great Spirit. John also used to go there to pray and

◀ John Elliott wants to protect his sacred mountain, LA'U WELNEW.

have a pipe ceremony with his nephew, before losing him, too young, to cancer.

But these days, John said, "It's very different. I was on that mountain fasting and people were asking 'What are you doing?' The beautiful little pools and stream up there are meant to be private, but are no longer private. That upsets our people. People are crying about that. Even if they're bathing in the dark hours of the morning, people sneak up there to watch them. It's really an awful thing they're doing … We need to have a sacred place like that."

John has been chair of the Saanich Native Heritage Society for several years, so he hears the concerns people have about protecting their sacred mountain; he listens and he has a plan.

"We have to declare it as a sacred site and then move to keep it sacred. Something has to be done. The younger people are ready to go there and protect the place. We can't live with dignity the way it is because that's our church. It is definitely a special place, one of the last places we know to be like that. I feel that there's a spiritual connection there. It is one of the Creator's sacred places. He made it sacred. We try to honour it. When you climb a mountain, it's something you go through. It tumbles you a bit, puts you in touch with the land."

I had heard fragments of this story before, but I was fascinated and strangely moved by John's words. There is something about his storytelling that makes me wait for each word. I imagine he is a good teacher. John has taught at LA'U WELNEW Tribal School since it opened in 1989, and every year he takes the grades 5 and 6 students to their sacred mountain; he tells them the story of the flood so the younger generation gets the chance to learn about and honour LA'U WELNEW first-hand.

"We're in a different kind of flood today," John said, "and the LA'U WELNEW School is our refuge." The tribal school curriculum includes Saanich culture, history and the local SENĆOŦEN language, first written down by John's father, Dave Elliott, and now taught at the school by John.

"The history of the land needs to be told in the original Native language, and we have to have our sacred sites." John would like to see a protocol set for the mountain for people to follow. Now, it feels "like they ripped the Holy Com-

▶ Tom Sampson with YAAS Mountain in the background across the Saanich Inlet, where he can see it every day.

munion out of our hands and took it away. I really think we need to allow people here to have a sacred place and the rest of it will follow."

John and his sister, Linda Elliott, both speak eloquently about the deep relationship the Saanich people feel with the land, the significance of the forest as a spiritual place, the need for a pristine environment for ceremonies and the importance of LA'U WELNEW, as "the holiest place, a sacred landmark." John said most of us don't truly understand the depth of this ancient relationship between humans and nature, and I think he's right, but I'm hoping it's not too late to listen and learn.

-▶-◄-

Tom Sampson's family home on the Tsartlip Reserve in Brentwood Bay is on a bit of a rise, facing the sea. From his carefully tended front lawn, Tom looks directly across Saanich Inlet to YAAS Mountain, a dramatic, all-encompassing view of the mountain he holds most sacred. He's a lucky man, in some ways. He sees his sacred mountain every day.

But he feels sadness too. "Look at the mountain. It's dying," he said, as we sat beside his garden looking out. He pointed out the old and new roads cut in the mountainside, and talked about his role in trying to prevent further development on YAAS during the Bamberton town-development project debate in the 1990s. He's glad that didn't go ahead but regrets the fact that development plans are again under way, and this time the opposition has been diluted with the promise of jobs for the local Saanich tribes. It's a common conundrum, but for Tom, it feels personal and disappointing.

"YAAS" means to give advice, to go there to learn and become disciplined, Tom said, and he has been going to that mountain all his life. Like most of the elders and community members, Tom has gone there for ritual bathing, for fasting and for other spiritual activities.

"We go to the land and see the beauty of the land and thank the Creator for sharing the mountain. It's a gift from the Creator."

As with LA'U WEL_NEW_, the First Nations people of the Saanich Inlet have gone for centuries to YAAS Mountain on the Malahat for healing, counselling and learning from elders. Birds and wild animals—deer, bears and wolves—have made it home.

"We come to understand life and to learn about the sacred place. The mountain was a sacred mountain that preserved all life."

Now, Tom too is worried. It's hard for him to sit calmly and talk about the historical significance and cultural uses of his mountain when his most pressing concern is its present and future. When he fought against the Bamberton development, he argued, "You're killing our highest spirituality," and he had support from both Natives and non-Natives. An articulate spokesperson, Tom was involved in the First Nations cultural heritage impact assessment prepared in 1997, and said then, "This mountain YAAS is who we are. This is our CHELENGAN, our birthright, our teaching, this mountain."[1]

The word "CHELENGAN" actually translates more fully as "teachings of the places where you come from," according to Tom, and it's a concept that is difficult for us non–First Nations to grasp. It has to do with place being an integral component of how people know who they are, and a repository of knowledge in and of itself.

It's an idea that is significant to this subject of sacred places, but it is problematical to know how to apply it in the non–First Nations context. We can't invent teachings we don't already have, much as we might like to. We can only try to understand, and appreciate the profound thought that land is so intimately understood, in a society based on oral tradition, that it and the storytellers are inextricably interwoven. The places themselves become part of the spiritual teachings.

As Tom put it, "This mountain and land is my ancestor. Just looking at it is enough. I see so many things ... but when I see it being destroyed, I get angry sometimes."

No wonder.

According to the 1997 assessment report, YAAS Mountain remains important to the Saanich Inlet peoples as a source of plants and animals for food, for materials, for medicines and for spiritual purposes. Tom took his young grandson to the mountain to teach him self-discipline, alertness and awareness.[2]

"All the people here feel for YAAS," Tom said, referring to the four Saanich tribes of the Malahat area. His people don't have a heaven: instead, "When someone dies, we say they've gone up to the Great Spirit in the mountains."

"It's not Malahat Mountain," Tom said, a note of frustration in his voice. That is the white man's name for YAAS. "They have to see it as YAAS. When you want to destroy something you change the name so it doesn't have any meaning."

Naming things correctly in order to protect, cherish, even understand them is an idea that affects our consciousness of the world. Changing a name has a profound effect. Ask any First Nations family that was renamed to make it easier for the Indian agent, or immigrant family that was renamed at the point of entry into North America. Tom said it's important to receive and know your name in your own language—in his case, in SENĆOŦEN.

"Your name tells you who you are, what you can and can't do, and to stay in your territory. It was sanctified."

Like the land. I asked Tom if he has a favourite spot on the YAAS landscape; he smiled and indicated the bluff at the very top, under the radio tower.

"I've said everything I've wanted to say about protecting that mountain ... This being a steward of the land is an every-second-of-the-day job."

9

Prayerful Places: Large, Small and Personal

⇢⇢⇢⇠⇠⇠

*I pray to the birds. I pray to the birds because I believe they will carry
the messages of my heart upward. I pray to them because I believe in their
existence, The way their songs begin and end each day
—the invocations and benedictions of Earth.*

TERRY TEMPEST WILLIAMS, in
Refuge: An Unnatural History of Family and Place

⇢⇠

O CCASIONALLY, like a force greater than nature, someone sweeps into my life with such enthusiasm that I feel temporarily scooped up into theirs, and happily roll along for the ride. In our very first phone conversation, Naz Rayani, in his irresistible, warmly engaging way, wasted no time inviting me to join his next group tour to the Ismaili Jamatkhana in Burnaby, BC. I'd never heard of a Jamatkhana ("meeting house"), but I love visiting spiritual centres of any kind. Plus, I had already been "nazzed," the term of endearment coined by those who have realized that, whenever Naz asks you to do something, to volunteer for the World Partnership Walk or to join him on an ecumenical adventure, it's impossible to say "No." So, of course I said "Yes."

For Naz, a Victoria pharmacist and community organizer extraordinaire, who was awarded the Order of Canada in 2006 for his outstanding volunteerism and community involvement, introducing others to one of his most sacred places has become an annual ritual. He has discovered that an excellent way to build

◄ Naz Rayani in the courtyard of the Jamatkhana.

interfaith bridges is by introducing people to the Burnaby Ismaili Jamatkhana and Centre, and he has personally accompanied over a thousand people for a tour of that stunning building. Naz started bringing groups to the Jamatkhana for "a vibrant day of exchange and learning" in 1994, and after 9/11, he says he has even more reason to do so.

The Jamatkhana sits inconspicuously in a mostly residential neighbourhood of Burnaby, sunk into the ground on purpose to keep its profile low. A spacious courtyard, gardens, cedar trees, flowers and a large fountain are almost hidden down a flight of stairs, but once discovered, lead to the entrance of the impressively designed Jamatkhana and centre. Traditional Islamic architecture and décor, employing geometric shapes, symmetrical layout, layering and patterns, include stylized Arabic carvings and calligraphy, tapestries on the walls and a magnificent open prayer hall.

The Jamatkhana intentionally reflects the influence of the West Coast: the domes in the soaring ceiling of the prayer hall allow views of the mountains; the carved Arabic panelling is reminiscent of our trees; and the crushed white marble dust on the front wall is meant to resemble the coral of the sea.

The building was officially inaugurated by the Aga Khan, one of a long line of Aga Khans and spiritual head of the Ismaili community worldwide (totalling about 15,000 in British Columbia), at a ceremony in 1985. Designed by well-known architect Bruno Freschi, who also designed the Expo Centre, which became Science World, it is truly, as the invitation to the tour stated, "one of BC's best kept architectural secrets." A gracious monument, it awed me with its artistic flourishes: minarets set into spiralling octagonal staircases, calligraphic design praising Allah adorning nearly every wall and, finally, the lofty prayer hall. Naz said Allah selected the 1,500 people who attend this Jamatkhana regularly as "special people" and envies them their good fortune.

During the tour, the group was told more about Canada's Ismaili Muslims, a liberal branch of the Muslim faith, whose spiritual leader stressed the importance of women's education even 100 years ago; today nearly 90 per cent of all Ismaili youth in Canada get a post-secondary education.

☥ フ フ ☥

I was impressed and surprised by both the building and the beliefs espoused within it. When I asked Naz more about how he lives out his faith when he's home in Victoria, he told me about his responsibility to include both the spiritual and the worldly in his life every day. That's his struggle, his personal jihad: "How can I walk in this world today, fully participate in it, but simultaneously keep my spiritual life intact?"

In his native Kenya, spiritual life is naturally interwoven with daily life, but here, "you have to carve out those times and moments." However, his Shi'a Ismaili Muslim faith provides an answer: a sacred *time*, whether or not you can make it to a sacred *structure*.

"We've been given the space of time between four and five in the morning," Naz said, explaining that, after the necessary six hours of sleep, at 4 AM, "The brain is at its lowest ebb; you've done your rest and work is farthest away. That's the hour you'll have the most success in reaching the Ultimate, and seeing the light. The light is within us, but covered with layers. You peel off the layers each time you pray and meditate, and one day, hopefully, you'll reach the kernel."

So Naz gets up at 4 AM and often meditates right in his computer chair at home, emptying his brain of other thoughts. "It's my time," Naz says, a quiet hour when he breathes deeply and slowly and meditates on one of the 99 attributes of Allah (God). About twice a week, his morning meditation takes place at the local Ismaili Jamatkhana Victoria on Esquimalt Road, where he goes for evening prayers as well, at least five or six times a week. "I sit down and have no space in my brain except for God."

At the same early-morning hour when Naz is up meditating and praying, Senator Mobina Jaffer—attorney, former refugee and long-time advocate for immigrant women, who is also Ismaili—rises to meditate in her North Vancouver home.

"I have created a sanctuary in my house, in the basement, in a particular room," she said, and she tries to keep it free of distractions. She has a mat and incense, very simple. She also goes to the mosque when she can but finds that, in her constant travels as senator, "everywhere I go, in my hotel room I find a spot to pray. I feel it keeps me grounded in meditation. The Creator is everywhere."

Even when she is travelling on airplanes, she has "time to meditate and reflect … No phone. No disturbances. I find I'm really able to go in and find inner peace."

I thought about the serene beauty of the Jamatkhana, and the quiet hour prescribed in the mornings, and asked myself if I felt connected anywhere to a place of communal worship, meditation and prayer. I realized there is one sacred place, a small, rather simple building that draws me back because of its impact on me and my family more than 25 years ago. I guess the older we get the more we understand the homing instinct, the need to return to the place that was meaningful to us in the past.

-+>-<+-

M AYBE MY journey was meant to bring me here—back to this living room of the home of our friend Ruby Wilson at Cape Mudge village on Quadra Island—pointing me in the direction of a place where past, present and future meet. In my believing-in-fate moments, I think this is one way I can listen to and learn from the pieces of my past. Quadra Island is one of those pieces.

I was a young mother when I first attended a service in the United Church at Cape Mudge, early in 1980, and I didn't even know what kind of church I was entering. But I knew, from the first time I heard Ron Atkinson deliver one of his richly woven Sunday reflections, that this was hallowed ground. The church, originally a mission church for the village, had been opened up to the entire island population, Native and non-Native, only a few months before I started attending.

Unknowingly, I was a part of this new inclusive congregation, an initiative that Chief Harry Assu felt worked out well.[1] It was the first time in years that I started going to church again regularly, recognizing something precious, maybe rare, right there in that humble, wood-frame church on this sparsely populated island. There was a sacred presence, a spiritual connection that transcended the ordinary; it was compelling, and I didn't want to miss it.

79

There have only been a few times in my life when I felt that glorious, heady assurance that the planets were aligning, at least momentarily, exactly as they should. I was, by good fortune, a part of such a time and place.

So was Joy Inglis, an author and anthropologist who has lived on Quadra since 1974 and is a specialist in coastal First Nations cultures. Joy is an energetic, articulate octogenarian who does her writing and research in her delightfully whimsical cottage with the banana tree in the front yard, adjacent to the ferry parking lot in Quathiaski Cove. After a lifetime of study, Joy probably possesses as much local knowledge and history as anyone on the island, and she knows where to find sacred places. One of them is the church at Cape Mudge.

Reflecting on her years of active involvement there with her late husband, Bob, Joy said it is "a place where many people on the island who wanted to expand their life experience and understand a meaningful philosophy of life, and people who loved one another, [came together] in a spiritual community. It was the first time ever that I had felt that wonderful feeling of belonging to a group of like-minded people. We were constantly raised in our thinking by Ron Atkinson. [The church] came to reflect our aspirations and reflected a beautiful setting."

The We-Wai-Kai people of Cape Mudge, part of the Lekwiltok Nation, built the mission church in 1932. Ruby Wilson, who was born in 1916, remembers her father working six days a week to help build it. Even though Christianity was the faith brought in by outsiders (missionaries who arrived in 1878), at Cape Mudge there has long been a feeling of ownership in the church, along with the belief that Christianity and the Native spiritual traditions could exist side by side. This eclectic thinking, challenging the norms of the time, seems to have worked here.

Ruby, her daughter Alberta and son-in-law Dan Billy talked with Russ and me about the church and its meaning to the village.

◀ (*Left to right*) Alberta Billy, Ruby Wilson and Dan Billy in Ruby's living room.
▼ Blending of Christian and Native symbols in Quadra Island United Church.

"All the old people felt that was their sacred place," Alberta began, and Dan chimed in, "We were brought up in the church and I loved it. Our people built the church long ago. I love it because of our old people."

Beliefs became intertwined, Alberta said. "The old people weren't Christians, but were very spiritual. They already had that [spirituality] ... but my granny learned to read by reading the Bible." Her grandmother, Louise Hovell, Ruby's mother, was able to simultaneously feel such a kinship to the church that she told her family, "When I die, I want my bell to peal for me," while at the same time reminding her children, "Don't forget about your dance, your song."

As we sat in Ruby's home, we were close enough to hear the church bell ringing midway through our conversation. We had the kind of frank, far-ranging discussion that takes place when friends meet again after a long separation. We talked about the sorrows and joys of life: the pride of watching grandchildren graduate from high school; the pain of losing a beloved daughter to cancer; the tragedy of the residential schools and the healing that is still needed; the delight of watching the next generations come along (Ruby has 16 grandchildren, 22 great-grandchildren and one great-great grandchild). We recalled when Ruby became the first curator of the new museum at Cape Mudge, built to house carvings and artifacts returned to the We-Wai-Kai people in 1979. And we talked about the role of the Cape Mudge church throughout their lives.

"I used to go in that church and just sit there in the front pew when I was really depressed," Ruby, who could no longer sit comfortably on the hard wooden pews, said." I could just feel that lifting off my shoulders, that lovely, peaceful feeling. Any day of the week, when I was really down and out, I would go there."

"The sacredness of that stained-glass window is really important," Alberta suddenly offered. Russ and I were surprised and pleased. Russ had been asked by Ruby in 1980 to design and create the large stained-glass window in the church in memory of her parents, James and Louise Hovell.

"It represents who we are, fishermen, with the cross [the mast of the boat] that holds the gears together, and Grandmother Moon takes care of everybody," Alberta elaborated. "I always pray to Grandmother Moon because I want her to take care of everybody."

"When people ask who did that window, I tell them, a really beautiful person. He didn't charge me much either," Ruby said with a grin.

The spirit of a place is often dependent on people too, and Ron Atkinson was a person uniquely able to understand what would work in this congregation, this setting. Ron served as minister at Cape Mudge twice, and remembered when he, his wife, Donna, and their sons Michael and Marc first arrived there in July 1972.

"I just felt, at last I'm home." Yet, it was a place where he had to start over.

"The Native people in the village, their approach and use of words, gave me a whole new being—the gift of a new consciousness. I had never had a congregation that was so quiet, a rich, warm silence. We didn't try to break it. A large part of the liturgy dwelled in that ground of sacred silence."

Weekly prayer meetings consisted of this comfortable grounding in silence, then "they would sing, slow music, full of a kind of remembering and dreaming," and after about half an hour, the congregation would lapse back into silence and expect Ron to say something. "I would find myself almost given the words."

Joy remembered that the silence in the church impressed her too. "When we went to silence, it was total. Maybe a dog would bark," she said, musing how rare that is in our lives full of noise. "Do you remember we used to sing 'the circle is unbroken'? I still feel it."

▶ Quadra Island United Church.

ARTIST: RHONDA RICHMOND, 2000

One of the tiny, bejewelled life moments that I recall was the evening when Elder Sandy Billy sang a hymn to us in his language, Liq̓ʷala Kʷak̓ʷala. He rose and stood at the front of the church singing, and at that moment we also heard a familiar squeaky-clothesline-like squawking overhead. I looked out the window beside me and saw a bald eagle circling lazily in the sky, lingering just above the church, adding its voice to the sacred song.

→>‑<‑

ALBERTA BEGAN AGAIN. "The elders held that place in really high esteem. It was their sacred place. But other elders said, we don't need a building, we can find the Creator in the forest … We had a spiritual connection to the Creator way before the Christians came … The land base was the sacredness of all the people. My granny said, 'You have to be respectful of the land. We're just visiting.'"

When we said goodbye to Ruby, Alberta and Dan that day, and took the ferry back to Campbell River, I felt that the visit had been a reclaiming, but more than that: it had given me a new insight into my past, putting it in context within the set of circumstances that came together to make that period of my life a truly sacred time and place.

I O

The Sacred Forest

-•>-•>-<•-<•-

*In my dream that hillside suddenly lived—weighted with sap,
burning green in every leaf, every scrap of it vital! Woods,
that had always meant so much to me, from that moment
meant just so much more.*

EMILY CARR, in *Growing Pains: The Autobiography of Emily Carr*

-•>-<•-

ONE OF THE outstanding facts of life on the coast is our proximity to the ancient trees of the old-growth forest. Logging has been the backbone of our economy for years, and most of the old trees are long gone. Concern is growing that we need to preserve the ones that remain. For our First Nations peoples, and for nearly anyone who stands next to a towering giant, the sacredness of these live beings is clear: big, old trees link us to the infinite, the ancient, to life beyond our lives.

Way back, cathedrals were designed to emulate the forests of Europe, and people were meant to feel as though they were walking into a sacred grove when they entered the nave. Now, by contrast, we talk about the trees being like a cathedral; in fact, one of BC's most appreciated and well-known forests is Cathedral

► Giants of Carmanah.

Grove, a magical place on the way to Port Alberni that features a stand of giant trees about 800 years old.

Cathedral Grove was the first old-growth forest I saw when I moved to BC. It was overwhelming, and perfectly named, a stand of huge, old trees stretching halfway to heaven, and one of the most accessible stands of virgin forest in BC. The poet Patrick Lane said old-growth forests are a "repository of deep wisdom" where he has found "tremendous peace." He has trees that he talks to, and feels "an immense psychological wound" because of the loss of our ancient groves.

Artist Robert Bateman, who likes to create hiking trails designed "aesthetically, which is also spiritually" in the forested areas near his home on Salt Spring Island, described to me one of his sacred spots on the Reginald Hill trail: an opening in the forest with an old maple tree creating a cathedral-like setting under a huge arch. He loves the volume of empty space under it, "a place to pray, think of hopes and dreams, or whatever."

Farther along the trail, he looks down from a rocky cliff to an area where the First Nations summer camps used to be (as a naturalist he can tell by the tall, vertical shapes of the second-growth forest reaching up for the sun) and imagines he's hearing the laughter of the women and children and men coming in from fishing.

He paused, then added, "I felt I was in a cathedral when I was in the Carmanah forest. It's the spaces between, something about the spaces that is important, not claustrophobic. I guess that's why I like mist, fog, snow: atmospheric stuff describes the space."

People often speak of Robert's paintings as sacred or spiritual, but he was surprised at first when his art was used in palliative care centres. It doesn't surprise me, and neither does his mention of Carmanah Walbran Provincial Park on the west coast of Vancouver Island. It's the forest primeval, a place where thousand-year-old western red cedars and the largest known Sitka spruce trees in the world are part of an ecosystem that has been undisturbed for literally thousands of years: a place where, as Leonard Cohen might say, "God is alive, magic is afoot."

United Church chaplain Henri Lock once took part in a well-publicized Tree of Life Celebration in the rainforest near the park. He stood under the canopy of an 800-year-old Douglas fir with hundreds of other people concerned about deforestation, feeling the roots and "phenomenal biomass" beneath him, while Victoria's Gettin' Higher Choir sang. It was, Henri said, a "profound, worshipful experience, one of the portals to the sacred, something much larger than ourselves."

We do have parks protecting some of our most magnificent sacred groves here in BC. The story of the creation of one of those parks is a good example of how far some people will go to protect and preserve the land they deem sacred.

The woman who caught the attention of the media with the greatest exposure, no doubt, is well-known environmentalist Briony Penn, who rode, Lady Godiva-style, through downtown Vancouver on a chilly January day in 2001 in a desperate last attempt to save her sacred place. To be that committed, that passionate, that desperate about the land is a beautiful thing. It's not everyone who would ride nearly naked through the streets of a city for a cause. And Briony is serious about our need to understand our relationship to place.

As she told me later, it is funny how you can meet and talk and reason and persuade for years, and get nowhere, but one carefully chosen publicity stunt ("I was freezing," she admitted) and the world takes notice. She worked for six years to save the land, which includes the largest remaining stand of Garry oak in BC, the last stand of old-growth Douglas fir on Salt Spring Island and the widest arbutus tree (and one of the tallest) in BC. That tree is over 300 years old, and Briony knows exactly where to find it. She took me right to it on the path through the forest of Burgoyne Bay Provincial Park, as we worked our way up to the sunny slopes beside the Garry Oak Ecological Preserve that abuts the park. Nearly 1,000 hectares are now protected as park and preserve in Burgoyne Bay, thanks to the Salt Spring community's efforts.

Given her background as a formidable eco-activist, I wasn't surprised that Briony's sacred place was a rare piece of the ecosystem, but I was curious about this particular location. "It's beautiful, peaceful, culturally significant and ecologically significant," Briony said, and it's a hot spot for songbirds, turkey

◄ Briony Penn on the slopes she fought to protect, now part of Burgoyne Bay Provincial Park

► Andy MacKinnon at Witty's Lagoon.

vultures, marbled murrelets and eagles. She also cherishes this spot because "hundreds of islanders" spent years, and raised a million dollars, fighting to save it. The higher the stakes, the sweeter the victory: it seems we can't fully appreciate things that come to us too easily. Just as any true pilgrimage must involve effort and sacrifice, the six-year crusade to save this land has resulted in a heightened appreciation of its intrinsic value. Now, finally, Briony can savour its beauty, secure in the knowledge that this protected watershed will not be destroyed to build 40 luxury villas, as was once proposed.

"I had to make a stand, from a gut level. I had no choice. You work from an intuitive level. That's all you can do ... I think I understand that absolute grief when your place is lost," she mused. "I think we've lost something when we don't have a special place." She understands the feelings of the Native elders who tell her about the sacredness of this area, from the dark, scary place beside the ancient arbutus tree, where huge boulders came down in an earthquake in the 1700s, to the sunniest, driest spot on the hillside. The juxtaposition of darkness and light appeals to her. A fifth-generation Salt Spring Islander herself, she doesn't want to live anywhere else, and hopes to pass along her love for this land to her children's children.

This sense of continuity, of multi-generational appreciation for the forests and parks of the coast, affects Andy MacKinnon's choice of sacred place as well. His children grew up with Witty's Lagoon Regional Park in Metchosin as their wild backyard, and to Andy, a biologist, this relationship has become a sort of sacred pact.

"An awful lot of our best family memories revolve around the park, and that's what makes it very special to me. I've also spent some very unstressful times in the park on my own, enjoying the seasons, the spring wildflowers at Tower Point,

the swimming hole at the end of the spit, mushrooms in the fall and the winter fungi." And the park's centrepiece, Sitting Lady Falls, which roared down into the lagoon, the water level higher than Andy had ever seen it, one winter's day when he and I hiked through the rain to see the falls.

The day we picked was a wild one, when the rainy season was in full force, but Andy was unconcerned. A seasoned biologist isn't put off by a little rain, or even a torrential downpour.

Andy's home is just beside the park and his knowledge of each bit of flora and fauna there is extensive. He stopped to point out witch's hair lichen, talked about the 160 species of birds in the area and paused at a Douglas fir that had toppled into the lagoon, to say that his kids loved that tree and used to race out on it and push each other off. Then he walked jauntily all the way out to the end of it himself: he couldn't resist.

Andy's feelings for this place are intimate, long-standing, protective. To choose one spot on Earth and know and love it this well seems almost a sacred act.

▶ Adele Curtis enjoys all parts of Francis/King Regional Park.

I recall reading an author who said if you find a place you like, the best thing you can do is to stay there and put down roots, and care about that place. That's what Andy has done.

A naturalist, and co-author of the classic field guide *Plants of the Pacific Northwest Coast*, Andy guides people through Witty's as part of a Talk and Walk series and is also actively working to develop a Blue and Green Spaces strategy to further protect the Metchosin area. He loves living beside this park. "You can go for a walk and have to avoid stepping in bear shit ... I can live here another 30 years and I can find new things in the park each year. It's a source of renewal and strength."

→>◄←

ONE DAY I received an email from Adele Curtis, who wrote, "I am a nature photographer and teacher ... Francis/King Regional Park has long been a special healing place for me. In my many hours alone in the park, time spent with family and friends, time teaching students, and time sharing photography with fellow photographers, I am reminded again and again—if I am quiet, open, receptive—something magic will be shared with me by the trees, the atmosphere, the pulsing life. As a nature photographer the earth under my feet at every step feels sacred to me. Every blade of grass, every pebble, every breath of wind. I never take this feeling, this recognition, for granted."

We met at Francis/King Regional Park a few weeks later, and the first thing Adele did was call me over to see, nearly hidden in the lush green ground cover, a patch of deep purple violets already blooming on a late winter's day. Adele notices the little things and is drawn to the woodland forest partly because of its subtlety. "You must look at all ... it's like my life. There isn't one magnificent thing: It's gentle and subtle and varied." I like that idea: the mosaic of small pieces forming a whole that is greater than its parts. God is in the details, they say, and as we walked through forested paths, Adele pointed out favourite plants like twinflower, with its delicate fragrance, and vanilla leaf, with its silvery white

blooms. She says that naming things helps you to notice things. If we can't name something accurately, as Tom Sampson also pointed out when he was talking about YAAS Mountain, it doesn't register in our world.

But along with the tiny flowers here, the park includes a forest that has been there for over 10,000 years (this fact earned it a place in *The Hiking Guide to the Big Trees of Southwestern British Columbia*). The Saanich people of the Coast Salish Nation have been sheltered by this forest for millennia, and harvested many of the wildflowers and berries for food and medicinal uses.

The Heritage Grove portion of the park has Douglas fir trees that are over 500 years old. We wandered in that area for a while, and I asked, "Why are old-growth forests sacred?"

"There's probably something in the air. That's the flaky answer," Adele teased. But we were both left to think about that. Because there is something here that is undeniable. It's a presence, a solemnity, a timelessness. Trees are one of the longest-lived species on Earth, so perhaps they soothe our unanswered questions about eternity. They may be the closest examples we have. And, when old trees do die, they become nurse trees for new saplings, so their nutrients are passed along to yet another generation.

Adele told me she comes here about every two weeks, because it reconnects her to nature and to "the deepest place inside" of her as well. She was at a

◄ Feast for the eyes at Pacific Spirit Park. PHOTO BY PILLE BUNNELL

▼ Snow in Pacific Spirit Park. PHOTO BY PILLE BUNNELL

transitional stage in her life at that point, a mid-life time of reflection, and coming back here, her "special healing place," seemed particularly important. We often return to our touchstones, our sacred places, at times when we stand on a threshold.

"There's an experiential thing that happens when I step into this forest, [something] spiritual. When I'm at the best of my photography, I forget about myself. It goes beyond Nature as therapy. The wall between me and the trees melts. And the neatest thing is when I show my pictures and someone else feels that."

The spiritual aura that big trees seem to exude is often a part of what draws us to them. In the Vancouver area, the location most frequently mentioned as a sacred place was also the choice of former Vancouver mayor and now Senator Larry Campbell.

"I go to Pacific Spirit Park when I need to centre myself. The trees, diffusion of light, and the silence always bring peace. You cannot explain definitely why one location can have this effect, but certainly spirituality plays a role."

My friend Linette Smith, a lifelong outdoorswoman who is lucky enough to live close to Pacific Spirit Park and who goes there almost every day, also considers the park her sanctuary. A recreation manager in North Vancouver, she said that entering Pacific Spirit Park is "like walking through a curtain into a totally different space. When I go in there, I don't like to talk. I like to go in there and just listen—to nature and to my inner voices. It's a wonderful, ever-changing feast to the eyes. A celebration. At the simplest level, observing nature helps us to feel more connected to something greater, and I think so many people in this neighbourhood feel this way."

11

Yuquot, Where the Wind Blows from All Directions

->->-><-<-

How wonderful are islands!

ANNE MORROW LINDBERGH, in
Gift from the Sea

->-><-

T HE DOCK IN Gold River was crowded when we arrived to board our vessel, the coastal steamer M.V. *Uchuck III*. In this isolated community about a two-hour drive west of Campbell River, a camera crew, actors and extras were milling about amidst tourists and members of the Mowachaht/Muchalaht First Nation heading out to Nootka and Kyuquot sounds.

The crew was in town to film the TV movie *Luna: The Way Home*, the story of the famous orca, or killer whale, that had befriended the boats and people of Nootka Sound, nuzzling up nose-to-lens to cameras, following alongside the *Uchuck* on almost every trip and recognizing certain Mowachaht and Muchalaht people individually. Sadly, Luna had strayed too close to a tugboat and been killed by its propeller a few months earlier. The making of the movie seemed to help ease the pain of his loss, a sort of honouring of the beloved orca.

There was a general sense of excitement on the dock—motion, the buzz of a town when something out of the ordinary is occurring and everyone feels a part

◀ Voyaging down Nootka Sound on board the *Uchuck III*.

of it. Russ and I and our friends were already exhilarated about our first trip to Yuquot (Friendly Cove), a scenic two-hour boat ride away on Nootka Island, and this carnival-like atmosphere only heightened our joyful anticipation.

There is something important about anticipation, which is closely related to intention: that is, how we prepare for and what we bring beforehand to a situation. Anticipation is one path to the sacred. A true pilgrimage always includes both preparation and the element of surprise: being ready to welcome the unexpected. Islands are often unpredictable: edgy, self-contained entities that seem prone to the mystical and miraculous.

I'd heard so much about the spiritual qualities of Yuquot already that I was predisposed to expect either a grandly hallowed experience or a disappointment that might be a measure of my own limitations, rather than of the place itself. I could feel my blood rush during the spectacular voyage to Yuquot, along the fiord-like coast with its densely forested slopes, where we saw a bear come down to the rocks, watched a grey whale that swam beside the *Uchuck* like a friendly guide and spotted bald eagles. It seemed a prelude to a symphony.

Certain places on the West Coast have acquired a sacredness that is pretty much universally agreed upon by anyone who knows them. Somehow, the strands of history, culture and natural setting combine so powerfully that it is almost impossible to go there and not feel the *genius loci*, or spirit of place. Yuquot is one of those places.

Sid Tafler, author of the article "Secrets of the Chiefs," which tells the story of the removal of the renowned Yuquot Whalers' Shrine (or Washing House) from its home on Nootka Island, readily admits he is under Yuquot's spell and is always amazed that relatively few people know about it, because for him it represents the spirituality of the West Coast at its most glorious. Historically, the village of Yuquot depended on the skills of the whalers; ensuring a successful

▶ Beach at Yuquot.

hunt by purification at the Whalers' Washing House—a place of such sacred power that for generations very few people ever dared set foot on it—was treated as a matter of life or death.

No one knows exactly how long people have lived on this wild and windy piece of land, but archaeologists have found artifacts on Nootka Island that confirm human habitation going back at least 4,300 years. The Mowachaht/ Muchalaht First Nation say their ancestors have been there since "the beginning of time" and believe that additional research will prove it was much further in the past that their ancestors arrived on that magical piece of land.[1]

We are awestruck by European monuments dating back a thousand years, and it is almost beyond our comprehension to imagine the civilization that could have existed on Nootka Island, and persevered, for over 40 centuries.

The only people now living full-time at Yuquot ("where the wind blows from all directions") are one Mowachaht caretaker family and the lighthouse keepers. Yet, the importance of Yuquot to the Mowachaht/Muchalaht First Nation remains—this is their homeland, their ancestral territory.

The experience of Yuquot is like sitting down to a large, intricately designed jigsaw puzzle and wondering which of these colourful pieces should be placed on the board first. So many sparkling bits of information.

History: Yuquot was the centre of the Mowachaht world, a thriving commercial and cultural base, and later the West Coast fur-trading centre for the Mowachaht people and the British, Spanish and American traders hoping to stake a claim on the area for their respective empires.

Nootka Sound is also recognized as the site of first contact on the west coast of Vancouver Island between the ancestors of the Nuu-chah-nulth people and the European sea captains, starting with Juan José Pérez Hernández in 1774, and then Captain James Cook in 1778. The first European adventurers arrived to a warm and friendly welcome (hence the English name of "Friendly Harbour," now "Friendly Cove"). The federal government has not once but twice declared Yuquot a National Historic Site, in recognition of the significance of its historic role to the Mowachaht people and to the Europeans.[2]

Spirituality: The home of the renowned Yuquot Whalers' Shrine, or Washing House, which was so sacred and significant that only high chiefs and their attendants were permitted access, for purification and washing rituals. The shrine and its artifacts, which included 92 carved wooden figures and 16 human skulls, were sold and carried off to the American Museum of Natural History in New York City in 1905, with anthropologist Franz Boas waiting with open arms to receive this treasure. For the last several years, the repatriation of the shrine has been a complicated ongoing discussion.

Conflict: The time of first contact in the late 18th century was also a time of cultural misunderstanding and conflict, as two very different peoples met each other. The reigning Chief Maquinna (the name has been passed down the generations) ultimately attacked the American merchant ship *Boston*, in 1803, and the only two survivors, John R. Jewitt, a British armourer and blacksmith, and John Thompson, an American sailmaker, became slaves of the chief (and were well treated) until their rescue nearly three years later.

Grandeur: The sweep of a huge pebble beach, the wild beauty of a rocky island, the thrill of the almost-certain sighting of whales even today at this historic whaling centre are coastal icons on an epic scale.

Continuity: Despite the tribe's relocation to a reserve in Gold River, most of the community members return each summer for a two-week campout in the large meadow above the harbour and stay for the annual August Summerfest.

Impressions: After exploring the island, staying in a rustic cabin overlooking historic Jewitt (*Aa-ack-quaksius*) Lake and taking part in the Summerfest, my overarching impression was of the rootedness of the people who, here at Yuquot, are comfortable hosts in their own ancestral home.

Richard Inglis, an anthropologist who has worked closely with the Mowachaht/Muchalaht First Nation for 25 years, and whose bond with the people and the land goes far beyond professional interest, also feels the spirituality of the spot.

"The land is sacred, in the broadest sense—a place of living history, of songs. The place does have power, no question, a spiritual sense," said Richard. "When we're celebrating the history of places, it's important to go out to those places to see where these events happened ... You have to visit it."

From the ridge where Ray and Terry Williams' house is located today, it is easy to imagine the time when a village of up to 2,000 people lived on that site, and when ships from Britain, Spain and the US anchored in the cove and surrounding waters more than 200 years ago. As the elders would say, when you're on the landscape of Yuquot, you're walking in the footsteps of your ancestors. It is a place that "tickles the memory."[3]

Richard and his wife and children visit Yuquot every summer to camp and experience the spot. For Richard, "the spiritualness of that place" is not dependent on the Whalers' Shrine, with its unmistakably sacred aura, but on something beyond that. He feels that Yuquot itself, where the narrow neck of land bordered

◄ Young visitors welcomed us at our cabin. (*left to right*, Jasmine Amos, Kayla Claywater, Beatrice Jack and Kyla Fred)

by a curve of windy beach on the exposed outside and a sheltered bay nestled on the inside, creates a calm beauty on the grassy field in the middle—is a "very special place."

"When I talk to people about the history of Yuquot, their stories are often beyond the events of history; they are very personal and many of those personal stories make my hair stand on end and poignantly point out that this is a place of power, a very spiritual place." Richard talked about stories like the well-known saga of the day an eagle washed ashore in front of a woman as a sign just after her husband had been drowned. This kind of story enters the spiritual realm.

Yuquot remained the main village of the Mowachaht people until the 1960s, when the Canadian government persuaded the community to move to the supposedly safer confines of the Ahaminaquus Reserve at Gold River. It turned out that that location, dangerously near the pollution from the pulp mill, was deemed unsafe, and the Mowachaht people were moved again, this time to their present reserve at Tsaxana.

The community's return to Yuquot each summer for the campout, grave tending and Summerfest is an important ritual. It was during the campout that a charming group of young preteens walked confidently up the steps to the tiny tourist cabin where we were staying and happily introduced themselves, saying they were going cabin to cabin to meet people.

I found myself thinking of the shy uneasiness of many First Nations children in our schools, and realized—of course these girls are comfortable here: this is their home and they are surrounded by their families and friends. We are the visitors, the ones out of our element. What a difference to meet people in their own territory, immersed in their own celebration.

When I mentioned this later to Bruce Lund, manager of Aboriginal Issues for Heritage Canada, his response was that Yuquot is "the kindest place to be on Earth" for the Mowachaht people, and each year, as their culture becomes better recognized, this confidence grows.

Terry and Ray Williams never left Yuquot and have become the resident caretakers of the island. When the other villagers were relocating, Terry simply

didn't want to leave the life she loved on the ancient land where her grandparents and parents had raised her.

Ray agreed. "We didn't ask each other. We just watched everybody leave without feeling left behind. Something was keeping us here. We don't know what, but I think it was our ancestors that wanted us to hold on."

Ray told me this over coffee in the living room of his home, stopping each time the two-way radio crackled with messages about the Summerfest to be held later that day. As a boy, he was sent to residential school, and he still carries the pain of that dislocation and trauma. His decision years later to stay in Yuquot with Terry, one of the few people fluent in the Mowachaht language, brought an unexpected benefit. It meant, Ray said, "I got my language back," a gift that is increasingly important to the Mowachaht and other First Nations peoples on the coast.

Terry goes for walks every day and faces the ocean every morning, stormy weather or not. She walks across the field and up to the rise above the expansive curved beach, where whales sometimes come to rub their bellies on the rounded pebbles.

"Our people belong here by the ocean. They're losing touch with our history. The kids love it here," she said.

Terry feels especially comforted walking on the path near Jewitt Lake; the Whalers' Shrine was originally on a tiny islet in the middle of the lake. Ray also

◄ The trail through the trees to the lake.

▼ Clear waters of Jewitt Lake.

loves the path through the trees, past the graveyard, to the lake. "There's something there" on that trail, he said, and others who visit the island often come to him to tell him they feel it too.

He also feels the presence of the shrine site and goes to the lake when he faces a problem, or illness, or wants to gain power for his carving (his son Sandford is a master carver). He and all of his children have ritually bathed in the lake, diving under for as long as possible, then emerging with a loud yell and listening for the echo that assures them their ancestors are working on their healing. "The presence of the echo is so striking that you'll feel the energy."

My husband and I also swam in the perfectly clear lake water, sometimes coming upon children meeting their friends for a dip, frolicking and laughing. We spent a lot of time trying to figure out exactly where the tiny island that was formerly the site of the shrine was situated. Somehow it was important to me to at least look over in its direction and know that my gaze was resting on the wooded ground of the sacred islet.

At the Summerfest later that day, huge portions of salmon, bannock and potato salad were served to all guests. There was traditional drumming, dancing and singing, and a series of elders, including the current chief, Mike Maquinna,

◀ Traditional dancing at Summerfest.

spoke and made presentations. Several mourned the passing of Chief Jerry Jack, a respected Mowachaht elder, who knew the history of Yuquot well and had recently drowned in a canoeing accident. Each loss of an elder, a guardian of history, is a blow to the community. The film crew we'd seen earlier in the day was there too.

The festival's theme, in fact, was "Tsux'iit (Luna), Strong and Powerful" and speeches lauded Luna, whom many believed to have been the reincarnation of Chief Ambrose Maquinna. When one visiting elder spoke eloquently of his feelings of being reunited with the chief as Luna laid his huge head on the man's shoulder, it seemed, in that wild, mystical place, easy to believe it could happen.

I had been skeptical, reading news reports of the supposed return of the chief, who had declared he was coming back as an orca shortly before his death, but now, to be honest, I don't know what to think. I do know I'm less likely to be so smugly dismissive of possibilities, of what we do and don't know for sure. Is there a link to the ancestors that is beyond the seeing of most of us? Is that what I felt momentarily in Skedans on Haida Gwaii? It seems unwise to rely only on empirical data when you are in a sacred place like Yuquot.

After the Summerfest, on the way back to Vancouver Island aboard the *Uchuck* on another exquisite summer's day, I thought about living in Yuquot in the storms of winter, all alone, sometimes not even able to take a boat to Gold River. I wondered if the Williams ever feel isolated, and then I remembered what Terry had told me.

"I never feel lonely," she said, because she can feel the ancestors with her wherever she walks on the island. "Living here all these years alone, it doesn't matter where we go now, because they're here. The connections are here."

1 2

Bernice's Synagogue

-+->-+->-<-+-<-+-

We make a building beautiful when we stop for it,
arrest the motion of thoughts, and linger with it.

ROBERT SARDELLO, in
Facing the World with Soul

-+->-<-+-

BERNICE PACKFORD is always happy to talk about the synagogue in Victoria that she loves so much. It's a treat just to listen to her—to delight in her passion for life, her astute observations of people and place and her pleasure in engaging in stimulating conversation. A chat with Bernice is a balm to the soul: you can't help smiling afterwards and believing that this old world will be okay.

Bernice is 92 now and it is impossible to imagine her slowing down. In one breath, she told me she's just out of hospital ("was in just three days, I'm so grateful for the calibre of service in Emergency") and went on to say that she finally, with appropriate pomp and formality, celebrated the completion of her 10-year plan to put a covenant on her 22 hectares of land in Sooke. The covenant restricts development of the land, which is now an ecological gift, to be managed in future by The Land Conservancy. Bernice held the ceremony right on the land, with her rabbi, Harry Brechner, officiating, which seems appropriate since Bernice is a woman whose faith and life work are inextricably intertwined.

Naturally, we talked about how things are going at her *shul,* or synagogue, Congregation Emanu-El. The oldest surviving synagogue on the west coast of North America, the building today is bursting with the energy of dozens of active, dedicated members—socially involved, talented people who make it what it is. But for me, the essence of this historic landmark can be distilled by listening to one member, Bernice Levitz Packford, tell her tale.

Bernice grew up in eastern Canada and moved to the West Coast 55 years ago. Her Jewish forebears were a tiny minority in Victoria, yet a group that played an integral part in the life of the emerging city in the mid-1800s. The city fathers of the day, including the Masons, who laid the cornerstone, joined with the Jewish settlers to build a magnificent synagogue. But first, following tradition, the Jews of Victoria established a Jewish cemetery, the oldest one in western Canada. The synagogue opened in 1863, eight years before British Columbia even became a province. This, by West Coast standards, is one old building.

So this is a story of two Victoria icons: the 145-year-old Congregation Emanu-El, and nonagenarian Bernice Levitz Packford, well-known community activist and esteemed member of the congregation. Their stories have become inter-woven over the years: Bernice is an institution within the institution.

It is inspiring to me to be around someone who is so rooted in her religious belief and community that she can accept, with equanimity and certainty, the imperfections of human nature, the shrinking and expansion of her congregation, the critical times of doing battle and the heady days of forward movement. Faith like this reminds me of a ship, probably an icebreaker, that steams along through the ocean regardless of calm or restless seas, of onboard infighting or political whims, of offshore dangers or unseen icebergs.

Bernice Packford provides an opportunity to see up close the way a house of worship frames and strengthens faith; it has become sacred to her both as a place of ritual and ceremony, and because it houses the community of believers of which she is an integral part. As Rabbi Harry says, the shul is not just a house of worship; it is a house of assembly. Congregation Emanu-El is a heritage building that resonates with history and welcomes the fluidity of everyday life. From the time I first entered its lofty space and sat in the balcony as the haunting klesmer music of a clarinet spiraled up to meet me, I could feel the power of place there.

Bernice insists that the remarkable willingness of early Victorians to embrace and support the Jewish community in the construction of this building was nothing short of "miraculous." Not just unusually harmonious, but miraculous. It's true that the surprisingly open-minded attitudes of the colonists who helped bring the synagogue project to fruition read like an ecumenical fairy tale of cooperation and tolerance. Large building fund donations poured in from non-Jews. A story in Victoria's *British Colonist* newspaper extolled the "high esteem" and "brotherly feeling" toward the Jews from "all classes of our community." French and German groups, the St. Andrew's Society and the Masons participated in the project. Can this sort of auspicious beginning linger in the very brick and mortar of a place?

Perhaps. Despite some lean years, when the Jewish population was declining and times were tough, Congregation Emanu-El never closed its doors, never stopped holding services.

"That has a great deal of meaning for me. It's history and I'm part of that history," Bernice said. When she attends services, she thinks of all the people who preceded her in that space. "They're in my thoughts when I go. No other building can have that ambience for me."

The sense of place, Bernice said, is "powerful … I get a feeling in that building, an aura." Decades of rituals and ceremonies have been performed there, including her daughter Leah's bat mitzvah. "It's crucial to forging relationships that we need repetitive ritual to keep reminding us, to strengthen us, to build our memories as we go through life."

The idea that repetitive ritual is part of a process that, over time, creates hallowed ground in a place is one I keep hearing, and it makes sense to me. Sometimes it may be the heart of holiness. Organized faiths recognize this, and it seems to be a characteristic of human nature that no matter how disorganized we are when

◀ Bernice arriving at her shul.

▶ Synagogue Emanu-El, Victoria.

we begin something, we gravitate toward the comfort and clarity of ritual. We may throw off the yoke, think of ourselves as revolutionary and new, and discard the recognized traditions, but give us a chance and we yearn to create rituals and begin traditions of our own. Often, that means recognizing that we need to create ritual at our sacred places.

Over a length of time, an energy seems to build up, as though we've worn certain pathways to the Creator simply through years of mental and physical activity repeated over and over in a spot. The neurons in our brains respond to the repeated use of certain pathways and that triggers strong, quick reactions—like the faster route to a website once you've opened it several times on your computer—so imagine all the brainwaves converging in a place of prayer.

Bernice has had the advantages of growing up in a faith already rich in tradition and being able to attend services at Congregation Emanu-El for more than five decades, since 1952. Every Saturday morning, she walks into the synagogue and slips into her usual pew on the right, third row from the front. It's the pew where her mother and sister also used to pray. This is her sacred place.

"I walk in there and the synagogue just suffuses me." Bernice is one of the shul's longest-serving members and has never wavered in her commitment. In November 2005, she was honoured there as the first recipient of the Ralph Barer Community Service Award. Bernice may feel that she couldn't have survived without her shul, but as her friend Ada Cotton said, "Without her, I don't think the synagogue would have survived the bad days ... There is no one in the synagogue who has more respect bestowed upon them."

Rabbi Harry Brechner added, "Bernice keeps us honest—she calls us on our stuff! As an elder, she is a moral compass. She reminds us of who we should be."

In the early 1980s, Bernice walked into the shul and saw the entire interior gutted. "There was nothing but the brick shell," she said, and she actually wondered if the venerable old building would remain standing.

The synagogue not only stood, it was transformed. The major restoration undertaken by the congregation at that time revealed the red-brick beauty of the original, Romanesque-revival style of architecture, which had been hidden for years behind stucco walls and a false ceiling. When the restoration process was completed, the synagogue reopened with a joyful community ceremony on June 6, 1982. In 1983, the 120th anniversary of the synagogue, Temple Emanu-El was declared a National Historic Site.[1]

"It was a dream that came true, a wonderful day," Bernice said. "The city cordoned off Blanshard Street and it was full of people," including the mayor and the premier. The evolution of the synagogue, from stability to fragility to renewal, reflects the history of the congregation itself.

"I never stopped going, because that's my place. That's my place," she repeated.

Bernice's lifetime pursuit of social justice, professionally as a social worker and personally as a Jew, is a weaving of the two strands of her life. Her public commitment to justice is nurtured spiritually and privately within the shul.

When she was a child, Bernice and her mother went to synagogue only three times a year, at High Holidays, since her mother could not afford to close her small business in Toronto at other times. Bernice remembers sitting high in the balcony, apart from the men, watching her grandfather below. Since she moved to Victoria, however, the weekly services at Congregation Emanu-El have become integral to Bernice's life.

"It's my place for thinking, remembering and sometimes even transcending myself," she said. "It's not a peaceful place, [but] even if I go and think of all these issues—and we've had some difficult, difficult times—people came along [to help out] at the right time, so that we have a future as Conservative Jews."

The congregation is now egalitarian, with men and women in equal roles, but, "It was a slow process. We didn't want to insult people who couldn't accept women going up [to the front of the shul], so we waited until people left this earthly scene," Bernice explained, a twinkle in her eye. "I know people who are looking, looking, looking, but they weren't brought up in it, and it's harder for them. I'm born a Jew, so that did help. I came here and stayed with it. I am so thankful and that is what I express when I go to the synagogue. I have the good fortune to live in Canada and Victoria and to have a community that I am a part of."

For Bernice, the synagogue is the place that gives her time for quiet reflection, for being with friends and for participating in the rituals that anchor her life.

13

Shared Sacred Spaces

-+>-+>-<+-<+-

*Certainty undermines one's power, and turns happiness
into a long shot. Certainty confines.
Dears, there is nothing in your life that will not change—
especially all your ideas of God.*

TUKARAM MARATHI, poet of India (1608–1649) in
Love Poems from Gods: Twelve Sacred Voices from the East and West
Translated by Daniel Ladinsky

-+>-<+-

HENRI LOCK arrived at the University of Victoria Interfaith Chapel one Friday morning to find a mountain of shoes filling the entryway. At least 200 people were at prayer, kneeling to face Mecca on their prayer rugs or on the large white sheets placed on the floor of the celebration hall. People spilled out of that room onto every bit of floor space in the chapel; the women gathered in the meditation room. Some of the faithful were even praying outdoors at the front entrance, as members of Victoria's Muslim community came together to celebrate Eedu-l-Fitr Day, the Breaking of the Fast at the conclusion of Ramadan.

Just another typical day at the chapel, a space that was created as an afterthought on the grounds of this secular university campus. But Henri, the United Church chaplain there, loves to recount these stories: they are part of the rich fabric of a shared sacred space that is particularly meaningful to him

Henri's relationship with the Interfaith Chapel goes back to 1992, when he and his wife, Leslie Black, came to UVic after five years as lay ministers in the

▶ Henri Lock outside the Interfaith Chapel at the University of Victoria.

Gitxsan village of Kispiox. Within weeks of moving to Victoria with his young family, including a toddler and a new baby, Henri was diagnosed with cancer.

"It was just like our whole world came crashing down on us," he said.

While Henri never gave up his job as chaplain, the impact that the illness and accompanying treatments had on him and his family was profound. During that time, Henri turned to the chapel and the surrounding gardens for solace.

"In this garden, during my cancer treatments, I would come just to find peace, to deal with the chemotherapy treatments, to let them drain into the ground, for a sense of healing and connection."

The Interfaith Chapel sits nearly hidden among the trees and growth of the lush Finnerty Gardens, a location that enhances the feeling of connectedness between the building and the outdoors: inner and outer nature. The out-of-doors is brought right into the celebration hall, a spacious gathering room, by the inclusion of giant greenery planted inside at the front of the hall. The sky is visible through a skylight about eight metres above, in the pyramidal roof of the building.

The UVic Interfaith Chapel, which officially opened in 1986, was designed to serve the widest spectrum of spiritual needs: a centre where people of all faiths, or none, could gather to find quietude in the midst of harried student lives. No religious symbols adorn this building: groups bring, and then take away, any icons they wish to display. Chaplains representing more than a dozen faiths, including Anglican, Baha'i, Baptist, Buddhist, Catholic, Christian Science, Judaic, Lutheran, Muslim, Orthodox Christian, Pentecostal, Salvation Army, Sikh, United Church and Wiccan, all share this space. And there is no denying theinnate feeling of spirituality, of sacredness, within the building.

"I really love this building because the materials that have been used are all indigenous, cedar, and the building flows to the garden and the garden to the building. It's a wonderful place to walk. That's part of the sacredness, not just the building, but the gardens," Henri said. "I see all the seasons change from the meditation room. In spring, the rhododendrons and cherry trees explode with colour; everything breaks forth, a very joyous time … [In winter], it's dreary and wet,

but fresh and green. Even in the dark time of year, the verdant energy flows in, vibrant. The sacred space is not separated from the natural space around it. It's one."

Wiccan chaplain Heather Botting-O'Brien said that at a meeting of the Interfaith Chaplaincy, there was general consensus that "having so many different traditions going through their rituals in that space has turned it into one of the most profoundly sacred spaces." The chaplains talked about this and agreed it is directly attributable to the fact that the chapel is a shared sacred space.

"There is a peaceful energy, a positive, not just the absence of strife— a mutual respect and understanding," Heather said. The chapel is also located on land considered sacred by the Coast Salish people.

Henri said of the chapel, "I return to this place again and again in order to find stillness." For him, a sacred place is a place "where the veil is thin and we see with our inner eye. This space really helps make that happen …When I walk in, I immediately feel the energy of what has happened [here], sadness, laughter, joy."

-+->-<+-

CANADA'S FIRST ecumenical church, where different Christian denominations and the Jewish community all held services, was built in a place that may be a surprise: Whistler, BC, the home of one of the best-known ski resorts in North America and a venue for the 2010 Olympic Games. There, a Norwegian skier named Franz Wilhelmsen (president of the company that first developed Whistler Mountain) helped establish the Whistler Skiers Chapel, which served

◄ Whistler Skiers Chapel in the old days.
ARTIST: ISOBEL MACLAURIN

► A quiet moment at Whistler.

the Catholic, Protestant and Jewish communities from 1967 to 2000. Who knew powder lovers could lead people to ecumenicalism!

Morgan Montgomery has been involved for years in the Whistler Skiers Chapel Society (which became the Whistler Interfaith Society) and is now chair of the board of the Whistler Village Church, which meets in the new Millennium Place in Whistler Village.

The Whistler Village Church is a unique, first-of-its-kind congregation made up simultaneously of three denominations: Anglican, Evangelical Lutheran and United, with a shared ministry to a diverse congregation. The Reverend William Roberts said the congregation at the Whistler Village Church is "almost a microcosm of the way the world is changing." As William sees it, in the postmodern world, there is no single narrative. The Christian story is "not the only story, but one compelling story." The Whistler Village Church comprises Christian traditions and is "a place where people come and there's endless variety and creativity that is worshipful and inspiring."

I was curious about where Morgan considers his sacred place in this ski town. He told me, "When I first came to Whistler, the sacred space was the Skiers Chapel, and the mountain itself. A lot of people go up on the mountain every Sunday, or other days, to a certain spot, and sit and commune with God— Frankly, I came to Whistler to ski, but I found you're more open to feeling the spirit and feeling God's presence when you're up there."

I liked his honesty. Being on a mountain, summer or winter, alone or not, can be a spiritual experience. Many times, I've stood in the cold silence of a ski run when no one was around, to listen to the wind and quiet, smell the sweet firry smell and breathe a moment of gratitude.

Morgan said there are plans under way to rebuild the Whistler Skiers Chapel, which was dismantled years ago to make way for development, as "the sacred space on the mountain," with a completion date of 2009. The new building will probably be at the top of Whistler Mountain, near the Roundhouse Lodge, and

will be used for services, weddings and special events. At 2,000 metres, that would be quite the venue.

We need dreamers and planners. This next story is about dreams, hopes and visions, and the people who are working to bring them to fruition: the optimists, the faithful, the ones who won't give up. This is an ambitious project in Vancouver to design and build a "shared house of worship and congregational home for a cross-section of religious and spiritual traditions." It seems more than coincidence that the Whistler Interfaith Society is a part of this alliance.

Reverend Louise Mangan and Rabbi David Mivasair share a vision and are leading a coalition of 16 faith groups that dream of building an InterSpiritual Centre at a yet-to-be-determined site in the city. Groups as disparate as the Birken Forest Buddhist Monastery Society, the Shree Mahalakshmi Hindu Temple, the Quakers and the Anglicans are part of the venture. For David, that's the most exciting part of the process. He envisions the centre as a "place for action in the world" and believes "all the people working on this are deeply attracted to their own traditions and they all have a view that transcends their own. We all know we're on a particular path that expresses a universal truth. I think of different religions as being different languages, different sounds or clarity, some more highly developed, and every language works for people and the more we can see the world through the different languages, the bigger world we see."

At the same time, David realizes that "many people are interested because they don't fit into a church or mosque or synagogue" yet realize that they need something too, a place apart, a sacred place. They are not exactly secular (if secular means denying the spirit) as much as they are "attuned to the spirit and seeking spirituality in ways outside the normal institutionalized framework."

"This group doesn't want 'brand loyalty,'" David said, but is "searching for a way to hold a consciousness of spirituality and rituals and stories." They want someplace to go where they can feel part of a communal spiritual experience. The InterSpiritual Centre can be a sacred place for them as well.

"I really believe that there is a movement of sacred energies, most palpable at the edges [that is, here on the coast]," said Louise, chair of the InterSpiritual Centre, who thinks "we have more room for diverse cultures partly because we are less institutionalized."

Louise believes that in this postmodern, post-denominational time, we're more open to "alternate wisdom," which encourages faiths to come together as we recognize the interconnectedness of everything. She says the West Coast is the perfect place for transformation.

From an architectural standpoint, are there certain design elements that are required in a shared sacred space? Louise mentioned six things her group has identified: a connection to nature, a sense of sanctuary, food, water, light and easy accessibility to spiritual leaders. The InterSpiritual Centre architectural committee and its architect, Mark Ostry, consulted with and surveyed more than 35 representatives of established religious and First Nations groups and has come up with a more detailed list of specific architectural requirements for the new centre.

One of the very first items listed was "an indoor labyrinth (could be part of a flooring pattern)." There's that labyrinth motif again, this time on an across-the-spectrum interfaith list. Louise said that request "emerged spontaneously from various traditions," and she thinks it arises from a desire to put less emphasis on doctrine and maximize the physical experience, or spiritual practice, "around the Divine presence." She said those who responded to the survey and who are actively involved in the InterSpiritual Centre tend to be somewhat self-selected: they are usually "at the progressive end of each tradition."

Another design element commonly requested by the participants was vertical and horizontal windows (lots of light) and, for nearly everyone, a connection with the outdoors for ceremonies. People wanted a structure designed to encourage community building and hospitality, and, Louise said, "the centrality of sharing a meal was 100 per cent consistent." Of course, she mused, there will be challenges when one faith forbids alcohol and another uses it for a ritual such as communion: this is where the underlying philosophy of tolerance and inclusivity will be put to the test.

"There was a sense that there needed to be smaller dedicated worship spaces for different faith communities and a larger common space," Louise said, which will be a challenge, given the high costs of urban space. Learning resources such as a library with a study area, a bookstore, an area for art workshops (like drum making), music and singing, and for physical movement like yoga and dance were identified. The group wanted meeting and group seminar areas with "space to support interaction and good communication."

A section of the survey titled "Entry Ablutions" pointed out the need to be prepared for both the putting on and the taking off—the removal of coats and shoes, the cleansing of face, hands and feet, the putting on of robes, tallith

(Jewish prayer shawl) and head coverings. There is also a need to separate the sexes for certain groups and to find the cardinal direction of Mecca.

Within the common worship area, there is a requirement for an altar or focal point, usually raised slightly, and a place to bow or kneel on a rug or carpet. Louise thinks the unifying shape of the circle will be important in the new centre, as people expressed over and over their "openness to a circular gathering."

The plan is for the new InterSpiritual Centre to be the home of many faith communities, whose congregational life will be based there in smaller worship areas, while at the same time all groups will share the use of a central sanctuary.

The location of the new centre is still not certain, but Louise said there is an "exciting conversation at this point between the InterSpiritual Centre and the Unitarian Church of Vancouver" about the possibility of building the centre on an underused portion of the Unitarian Church property on 49th Avenue at Oak Street.

As Hardial Singh Garcha, President of the Guru Nanak Spiritual Resource Centre Society in Vancouver, told me, at one time this sort of thing—many faiths planning a building together—would have been impossible. Now, with so many interfaith dialogues happening, it could be a good time.

"I'm hopeful that it will go through. Major groups are merging with each other—banks, political parties—why not religious people?" Hardial said.

For David Mivasair, the question is, "Will this building allow me to feel God's presence more than elsewhere? I do think so, very much, with all our energies together." David has a "beautiful vision" of a building where he can be deeply engaged in his Jewish practices right in the same space where others who follow different paths can be as deeply engaged in their particular ways.

"It's really about opening our eyes, opening our hearts, opening our soul to where we are. It's our attunement to what is there that makes it a sacred place."

By sharing sacred spaces, those involved are making a hopeful statement: that people representing a diversity of faiths and beliefs can not only co-exist, but be strengthened by coming together under one roof.

I4

Providence Farm: A Place of Compassion

✦➤•➤•◆•◆

It is in the shelter of each other that the people live.

Irish proverb

➤◆

PROVIDENCE FARM in Duncan, BC, is one of those spots on the Earth where the word "inclusive" could have been coined. If you've got a good idea, and especially an idea that involves a group that is underserved or on the fringes, the farm may be just the spot to bring it to fruition. It is a place where people are warmly welcomed no matter what challenge they face in life and no matter how marginalized they may feel elsewhere. It is a healing place known internationally for its innovative programs for those dealing with mental health issues and developmental challenges.

Groups of all sorts have found a home at Providence. In 1986, for example, the Multicultural Women's Group of the Cowichan Valley Intercultural and Immigrant Aid Society needed a "studio" where they could set up and tape their newly launched cable-TV show *Kitchen Culture: the Multicultural Cooking and Lifestyle Show That Is One of a Kind*. Someone suggested asking Jack Hutton at Providence Farm, and that was the beginning of an unforeseen partnership, with

▶ View of Providence Farm.

women arriving at the farm each week carrying exquisite Thai hangings or colourful Mexican dishes up the stairs into the rambling old kitchen of Providence House, followed by volunteers lugging cameras, lights and sound equipment.

Providence had its 15 minutes of fame, a half-hour actually, when VisionTV featured the farm on its *Recreating Eden* series, as "an emotional and spiritual home for all sorts" of people. After the show aired, a woman in Ontario called the farm and wanted to move to Duncan so that her son, who had schizophrenia, could be part of this therapeutic community that, as far as she knew, couldn't be found anywhere else in Canada. That's the sort of place it is, a place that comes close to being the way the world should be.

Years ago, Jack said his goals were to "work here on the farm until I retire, and then work here on the farm for as long as I can." Sounds a bit like the enlightenment quote:

> Before enlightenment
> chopping wood and carrying water
> After enlightenment
> chopping wood and carrying water.

Jack also pointed out the right livelihood quote, which hangs on the wall of Providence House and reads in part,

> When there is no need for separating what one does from what one is
> When one's work adds to the reservoir of positiveness in the world
> that is Right Livelihood.

And then Jack would probably have added, "Anaways [that's a Jack-ism], people find right livelihood here on the farm, and that's why they keep coming back."

Yet Providence Farm and the wide-ranging activities carried out there somehow never have the heavy saccharine scent of the do-gooder. Instead, on one of

the most glorious patches of land on Vancouver Island, with Mount Tzouhalem ("*Quw'utsun Smeent,*"[1] a mountain sacred to the local Quw'utsun people) rising protectively above, forests bordering the lowlands, berry patches in the meadow, and rows and rows of richly tilled fields of crops, the feeling is one of a community working together tenderly, productively, proudly.

Several years ago I interviewed participants in the Greenways Therapeutic Horticultural Program at Providence, many of whom were dealing with schizophrenia. My lingering impression was a feeling of admiration, almost a gentle wonder, at the atmosphere of respect that permeated the farm. One of the men working in the fields told me, "Do you know what I like about working here? When I'm here, I'm not ill. I'm just an employee."

Another, crouching in a tangled mass of vines while searching for ripe cucumbers, added, "If this is what it feels like to be normal, I love it."

It was no surprise that Jack Hutton, mental-health specialist and born-again farmer, conceived of the Greenways horticultural-therapy program and snagged a grant from B.C Mental Health to get it started in 1984. It has grown to include market gardens, field crops, a nursery, greenhouses and a general store, well supported by the local community, selling organic produce.

The Providence Farm Mission Statement (how often do you see a mission statement worthy of quoting?) says in part, "Our focus is toward those not easily accepted elsewhere." The good nuns, the Sisters of St. Ann, who own the property, still take an active role in overseeing it, but long ago turned over the helm to the board, staff and volunteers of the Vancouver Island Providence

◄ Jack Hutton at his favourite place, the farm.

Community Association, the dedicated people who work on this 160-hectare property year-round.

The idea of Providence Farm is built on the whole concept of community, but few people would argue that Jack, usually found in cowboy hat and boots, has for years been the linchpin. He persuades by example: he loves the farm, believes in its mission, enjoys each person he meets there, and will grab a shovel and tackle the manure pile anytime.

In a former incarnation, Jack was the director of the mental health branch of the government in Duncan, sitting in an office trying to figure out how he could improve his own and his clients' mental health by getting out in the sun and working the land. He found a receptive audience with the open-minded Sisters of St. Ann.

He and Sister Frieda Raab came up with a plan, and this land, so swoopingly open and idyllic, was the catalyst. Thirty years later, the Sisters of St. Ann, Sister Frieda included, want the communal use of the farm to be continued indefinitely and are thinking of signing a 100-year lease with the Providence Community Association, which has operated the farm since 1979.

Frieda says that Providence is "much more than a farm. It's a spiritual quest for people. It's a welcoming place because of the people, combined with its historical roots, its tradition. All of these people here have a deep spiritual drive, if they recognize it or not."

The Sisters of St. Ann ran an orphanage, then boarding schools for local First Nations girls and later boys, at Providence until 1965, and the spot has been sacred to the Quw'utsun people for many generations. In 2007, a ceremony attended by the sisters and Quw'utsun elders was held on the property to honour its past, present and future uses. Quw'utsun cultural advisor Ron George was there to barbeque the salmon for the group of 80 elders, sisters, Providence staff and board members.

"The elders thoroughly enjoyed that day. The whole reconnection of meeting with old friends," he said later. He spoke about the sacredness of the site and the "in-depth feeling" it evokes in the Quw'utsun people. He mentioned the ancient relationship with the trees, especially the Garry oaks, and talked about how his people have always revered the connection to nature. It seems this land has been sacred forever, and somehow that essence has been tapped and carried forward in its present uses.

Now, a younger generation is carrying on with the work of Providence Farm, and the spirit of place remains. Jack said it is "an energy. And that's God-given … The setting is unique. Just tune in to trees, clouds drifting across the mountains, it's magical. You come here and it's quiet, a place of peace. If there was ever a therapeutic milieu, this is it. The setting here absorbs so much energy and gives it back."

Providence is home to an eclectic mix of activities: from the Cowichan Therapeutic Riding Association, which serves more than 100 handicapped riders a week, to the Cowichan Valley Alternate School and the St. Ann's Garden Club. Along with vocational and therapeutic programs, Providence hosts the Islands Folk Festival, an annual three-day music festival drawing crowds of more than 2,800 each day, and has community partnerships with groups like the Concenti Singers (who practise in the recently renovated chapel) and the Cowichan Bonsai Club. There are even plans and dreams to build a village on the property someday, affordable housing that Jack envisions as "an integrated, diverse community of seniors, people with special needs, and families" living together in a "supportive community that looks out for each other."

Aly Stubbs, the farm administrator for 20 years, knows nearly every foot of the property. She and Jack, the farm's executive director Mark Timmermans and I chatted in the warmth of the big office of the old house one morning.

"We all have a passion for the place. It looks beautiful. It chokes me up," Aly admitted.

As we talked, I could feel the nascent sense of longing that Providence always gives me: a desire to linger in this place. That is partly because I have a history with the farm, but it has to do mainly with the spirit of place and spirit of community of Providence. As Frieda put it, "People say, when I drive in that driveway, I feel a peace."

"The setting is as important as anything," said Mark, part of the new generation that is carrying on with the mission of Providence, "a feeling of camaraderie, [people] with similar values, working together ... There definitely is a very real spiritual blessing that has been given to this place ... That spirit of openness to the needs of the community."

Jack added, "The farm provides continuity. And has done that for a lot of people for a lot of time."

Continuity is often the thing that is missing in our diasporic lives, and is often an ingredient in creating a sacred place. When I arrived for a visit, Jack took me first to the lunchroom to enjoy the results of the group project of the morning: cooking up the midday meal for all comers in the newly renovated kitchen. He introduced me to everyone who happened to be sitting down to eat at the long tables, often providing a good-natured one-line description: "John's worked here for more years than any of us can remember!" No one was identified as client, staff, volunteer. Labels don't apply.

The philosophy at Providence seems to go roughly like this: we are all God's children, equally worthy of respect and dignity, each able to contribute to our community in our own ways, and each enriching our community by our part in it, so let's work and learn and laugh together on this protected piece of Earth.

At Providence, people have the opportunity to be the best they can be, in a safe haven. That's what happens sometimes in a sacred place.

15

Retreat

-➤-➤-➤-◀-◀-◀-

For a tree to grow and bear fruit, its roots must be deep in the earth.

MARIE ANNE BLONDIN, Founder, The Sisters of St. Ann

-➤-◀-

A S CHURCH ATTENDANCE in BC declines, other places that encourage spiritual growth have started to fill the gap. In the last several years, retreat and meditation centres have attracted people regardless of religious beliefs: basically, anyone who is seeking spiritual fulfilment or answers to the big questions.

My friend Sharon was the first person to talk to me about Queenswood and how she loved it as a sacred place. She had gone there for the 12-step program to help her through her alcoholism, and had great affection for the "awesome" nuns who had been there for her during that time.

People go to Queenswood, a centre for personal and spiritual growth nestled in the trees of Cadboro Bay, Victoria, for surprising and sometimes life-altering reasons. For example, Pamela Porter. She started writing at age 15, and decided in university that she would be a writer. In 1995, she was living in Deep Cove with two young children and a work-at-home husband, the phone constantly ringing

and the laundry looming. As an aspiring author, Pamela knew, and her husband Rob could see, she badly needed a "room of her own," a problem common to many women writers. It was Rob who first took the initiative to look for a place where his wife could go to write. That's when Pamela discovered Queenswood, and the quiet, welcoming library there.

Sister Audrey Beauvais, the librarian who became both mentor and friend, met Pamela and asked her, "What are you interested in?"

"How the extraordinary breaks into ordinary life."

Audrey was no doubt pleased. Her philosophy is that our searching is important. "If you miss the point of searching and finding something new every day, you really haven't lived."

She put a small desk in a corner of the library for Pamela, helped her find books she needed, and greeted her warmly every week for what turned out to be years. Pamela would sit in the corner and write, fervently hoping to get something substantial published in book form, partly just to show Audrey that her patient hospitality wasn't being wasted.

Ten years later, in 2004, Pamela's first book, *Sky*, was published. *The Crazy Man*, also written in the corner of the Queenswood library, followed in 2005, and promptly won the Governor General's Award for Children's Literature, establishing Pamela's reputation as a nationally known children's author.

◄ Pamela Porter (*right*) with Sister Audrey Beauvais in the Queenswood library.

When she thought about her years at Queenswood, her sacred place, Pamela said, "There is a special sense there—a particular kind of peace that can't be explained. A lot of people find some kind of grounding there and begin to blossom. The sisters, by their presence and spirituality, have created much of this."

Pamela also remembered how important it was that someone believed in her, understood the fact that she needed a place to write and willingly gave her the space to do so. And there was something else, what she calls the "spirit of silence."

"The depth that one can go to in silence is just the depth one needs to be a writer, and at Queenswood, I realize how easily one can get to that spot at that place. It's very deep. A depth you don't get to in busy everyday life. A depth you can get to that is profound. I've stood on mountaintops where no sounds could be heard except the wind, and waited for my heart to quiet. That is often the place I feel closest to God. But silence and quietness are scary places sometimes. Lots of people are not ready for that—you don't know what it will show you." For Pam, "It's been a real gift in getting my work done and being able to open up in that space where those characters would be willing to talk to me."

Silence and quietness. We say we yearn for them; we often choose sacred places where we can find them, yet, as Pam said, we're afraid of them too. Without the clutter, when we face ourselves quietly and listen for the inner voice, how do we know what we will hear? Sometimes the thought is so frightening that it is wise to do this in a safe or sacred place. Queenswood Centre (described in its literature as "An Oasis for Seekers") provides an environment that enables people to face deep truths about themselves, often at times of despair or suffering, and to find ways through the pain.

Monique Roy remembers precisely when she hit bottom in her life. She was unemployed, homeless, struggling to get along in English, broke and far from her Quebec roots. In April 1997, "I went to a place of darkness. I was really low, emotionally, spiritually, physically, financially … And I didn't want to live, honestly. It was a Friday afternoon and I was at a friend's house, because I didn't have a place to stay."

◄ Stained-glass window in Queenswood chapel.

But she knew about Queenswood and had been there with a friend to a 12-step program in the past. She finally called the reception desk and asked if she could stay for a few days.

"That was the only place I could find peace, and heal." Monique couldn't afford even the modest fees, but her offer to volunteer there in place of payment was turned down by the director, who told her to just "come and rest."

"There was a light at that moment," Monique said, as she let the tears flow. When she arrived that evening, she was welcomed by a kindly receptionist who had stayed late to greet her and say, "I was waiting for you."

"She walked me to my room," Monique said, "and my name was on the door, and there was a little flower with my name—and I cried, because I felt so shitty—so down and not worth it. And there was somebody who was there at that moment for me ... That moment has been the beginning of my healing. I had to go to that place, so low, in order to come out ... and it started at Queenswood.

"I touched humility instead of humiliation. Where humility kicks in, we are open to the sacred, and in that gap, the miracle happens. I spent the night from Saturday to Sunday in the chapel because I couldn't sleep. I spent the night on my knees, crying."

The next day, Monique spent hours talking to Sister Pauline Cormier, who spoke French. Monique knew she was "at the right place, with the right people, at the right time. I'll never forget this moment."

The Queenswood chapel is still Monique's favourite place, and she continues to take part in the weekly meditation circle. She has recently graduated from a counselling program, and has her own housecleaning business, which she says she does "with all my passion to bring joy" to the sacred space of others.

She returns regularly for retreats at Queenswood and loves coming upon the statue of St. Ann glistening in the sun at the end of a quiet path.

"Each place is my invitation to my conscious contact with my higher power." The milieu is sacred to Monique because of the beauty of the natural setting, "but mostly [because of] the love, the energy of the sisters," who are "non-judgmental" and exhibit "such transparent joy."

Monique called Queenswood "the house of my soul. It saved my life … This is the place where I can feel my inner strength. Even if I'm low, I can be who I am … We feel that when we come here. You know, it's …" she paused, "it's love. That's what it is."

-+>-<+-

SISTER PATRICIA SHREENAN stopped, mid-stair, on the steps in front of Queenswood on a blue-sky day that whispered of fall, engrossed in conversation so animated that she didn't notice she was perhaps in a rather precarious perch.

"In my 11 years here, literally hundreds of people have revealed themselves to me—in private conversation—and so my sacred space is really the people who come here … Almost without exception, I have those moments in the presence of another, almost always through a suffering the other is moving through. There is something sacred about the exposure of that suffering."

According to Patricia, the majority of people who go there for programs or retreats are not Catholic; in fact, they have no faith tradition. Queenswood, which Patricia described as "a place to reclaim one's own spirit and purpose," is open to everyone: men and women, seekers of all kinds. A staff of 23, including six Sisters of St. Ann, welcomes hundreds of guests annually. While the sisters own and administer the centre, and there is clearly a Christian orientation, Queenswood is "a place of welcome and inclusivity" for all people, said Charles Joerin, Manager of Spiritual Care for the Vancouver Island Health Authority, and a long-time participant in Queenswood's programs.

Charles explained the sacred quality of Queenswood by saying, "Certain places have an aura of spirit, of peace, of well-being, and the grounds and buildings of Queenswood have it … Lots of people have made life decisions there … that have formed them in their relationship to their God. Queenswood has a spiritual care history to it that has infused it."

For me, the immediate attraction to Queenswood was the warmth I felt from Sister Patricia and each person I met there. The ambience there provides a sanctuary that allows people to be alone or in communion with others. I was reminded that there are many paths to the sacred, often starting from a place of pain. Does this sort of revealed truth and recognition of suffering, divulged in an atmosphere that is safe and non-judgmental, imbue a place with sacredness? Many believe it does.

"Patricia's mentoring," said Debra Caravitis, an active participant in the Women's Spirit Space program at Queenswood, "has been a very important part of why this is sacred." When Debra suffered the tragic loss of her daughter several years ago, Patricia conducted the memorial service in the Queenswood chapel. And it was there that Debra started to heal. She returns to Queenswood, which she considers her "spiritual home," regularly, often to walk the labyrinth, and said, "A sacred place taps into the mystery of life. For me, there's an ancient, mysterious connection that I can feel."

-+>-<+-

A NEWER RETREAT CENTRE, which stretches over about nine hectacres beside the ocean in East Sooke, BC, is Glenairley Centre for Earth and Spirit. Glenairley's beach is on an ancient midden, where layers of crushed shells represent thousands of years of shellfish harvesting. More recently, the land has been the property of the Sisters of St. Ann, and served as their recreation area and swimming spot back in the days when nuns wore full habits. Sister Sheila Moss remembers the good old days when she would take off her habit, cover her swimsuit with the requisite black apron, and go to the beach to swim.

"I loved it always," Sheila, an avid swimmer, said. Today, Glenairley has become a non-profit ecological learning centre, run in partnership between the Sisters of St. Ann and the Centre for Earth and Spirit.

The property includes a wetland area where Keely Bays worked for several months on a wetland restoration project when she was a student at the University of Victoria. She said the project "created a bond with the land that I'd never experienced before." She had heard of eco-psychology and that being on the land could be healing, but it wasn't until she spent time at Glenairley, after taking a UVic course in ecological restoration, that she began to appreciate what that meant.

"I hadn't connected ecology with my spirituality," Keely said, but after replanting the Glenairley wetlands with native species and spending lots of time "hanging out in nature," she began to feel she was playing a part in restoring the "human–land" connection. She feels an emotional and spiritual link to the Glenairley property and believes the things they do there help people realize the connection between themselves and their environment.

"Centres like Glenairley are the next step in our connecting to the planet," Keely said, and she believes so strongly in the centre and its mission that she is now a board member. Glenairley "allows people to experience the interconnectedness of everything ... so we'll act in ways that are helpful to the Earth."

That idea was often expressed to me as I worked on this book. It seems that many of us are on a similar path, hoping that, in the 11th hour we live in, there is still time to find ways that connect and bind us to each other and to the Earth. People are recognizing that the planet is ailing, and we have to protect it by reconfiguring our relationship to the natural world, sometimes in a sacred contract. Places like Glenairley are making it easier to do that. Here, people practise what they preach and employ ecologically sensitive gardening techniques to attract insects and birds.

Keely's favourite place on the property is in the riparian zone, beside a stream in a small valley with fragments of old-growth forest. Sunlight shines through the giant maple leaves there with a golden glow.

▶ David Drysdale on a favourite perch at Hollyhock.

✦➤◄✦

SISTER SHEILA, dressed in regular street clothes these days, has been vice-president of Glenairley's board since it was formed in 2003, and said the Centre for Earth and Spirit is the "theological thrust of the day, and the future. Catholic theology has tended to be categorical. This you do. This you don't. But I believe God is not a part, God is in the centre. God is in all that is. We are one with all that is. It's a whole different way of looking at creation. Our role is to celebrate, protect, encourage, not to use and abuse."

Sheila talked excitedly about the future, firmly believing that Glenairley is a place where creation spirituality (not to be confused with creation*ism*), a "wondrous creative force" that recognizes the presence of God's spirit unfolding in all that is—the Earth, the Universe—can be experienced.

✦➤◄✦

PEOPLE COME TO Hollyhock to get away, to be rejuvenated, to learn about themselves and sometimes to seek the sacred. This ruggedly scenic retreat next to an isolated beach on Cortes Island, BC, is an educational centre that aims to "inspire, nourish and support people who are making the world better."

Hollyhock provides a supportive wellness community that encourages spiritual growth and personal transformation. Is it sacred?

I'd found a workshop in the calendar that seemed quintessentially "Hollyhock," a session on shamanism and "spiritual initiation." Since the course description made me a little uneasy, I realized that despite my alleged openness to spiritual pilgrimage, my comfort zone was perhaps smaller than I liked to admit. So I asked Hollyhock operations manager David Drysdale, who grew up in a small town near the ocean in Scotland and first visited Hollyhock 20 years ago, what makes this centre a sacred place to him.

"It's a combination. The land itself holds such an energy, an ancient energy, its tribal roots ... We're the holders of the crucible and set the space. And you set

your experience ... A sacred space is a space that gives you permission to be all you are ... It's intentionality, to provide a space where change can happen.

"A lot is the history. On an energetic level, all that's gone before is still here. The reverence for the land still exists." People who come there realize they are in a place that gives them space. "It's not in the words. It's in the spaces in-between, " said David.

Last year, VisionTV filmed a five-part series called *Five Seekers*, a sort of reality show for people on a spiritual quest. One of the segments was filmed at Hollyhock, and David, who had some doubts about the experiment, said he sat and talked to the participants, and "some of it was pretty woo woo for the people on the show," but "some of it was life-changing."

When I asked David if he had a favourite sacred place at Hollyhock, he suggested a walk in the woods. "Connecting to the trees is connecting to the ancients. I walk in God so deeply in nature or in my garden. This is church."

The two instructors of the shaman workshop, Richard and Donna Perez-Venero, said much the same thing as others had mentioned—that sacred space can be created anywhere, through ritual and intention. They use rituals in their sessions to make the space feel safe, and they call on the ancestors to help people "touch the mystery." Richard said there is a fundamental yearning for spirit not mediated by a priest; people want to dive right into the experiential themselves.

Their word choice was a bit different, but maybe the paths we are walking through the woods, whether in Queenswood, Glenairley, Hollyhock or our own backyards, aren't all that different after all. Marie Anne Blondin, the founder of the Sisters of St. Ann, would no doubt be happy to see how the desire to feel rooted, in the earth or in community, draws people to retreat centres in increasing numbers even today.

16

Sacred Waters

-+>-+>-<+-<+-

The voice of the sea speaks to the soul.

KATE CHOPIN, in *The Awakening*

-+>-<+-

WATER AND FORESTS are probably the most commonly chosen categories of sacred places people have talked about, which makes sense, living as we do on the West Coast. And of course water—essential for life—has been considered sacred around the world by nearly every culture and religious group throughout the ages. It is a symbol of grace (used for baptism in the Christian faith), purification or cleansing, or a reflection of the soul. The modern-day pilgrimage Sharon Hall and I made to a waterfall is an ancient ritual in Japan. In BC, where our livelihoods often depend on the sea, Charlotte Diamond's story seems a good place to begin.

Before she became the popular children's singer and songwriter she is today, Charlotte, then a young teacher, joined her fisherman husband, Harry, on his boat, the *Papillon*, every summer. She loved exploring coastal nooks and crannies, and going to places like Masset, Namu and Calvert Island. Both Charlotte and

Harry still feel the special relationship to the sea earned by those who have lived, worked and even died there.

Given this background, Charlotte's choice of sacred place is not surprising. The Fishermen's Memorial at Garry Point in Steveston, right beside the Fraser River, is the place she goes to, alone or with Harry "to stop, a place where you don't want to walk on.

"We all really need places where we go to find that solitude in ourselves, a feeling of reverence, things that bind us together, the Almighty," Charlotte believes. "Our society is so fractured. It's nice to find a place to relax, sit and feel connected to something greater than ourselves ... As our lives go on, places that are sacred to us become more and more important. They are touchstones. They are places where we go back to remember who we are. We need to celebrate who we are."

Charlotte admitted, "Never did I think this would be a full-time career." But since the release of her first album, *Ten Carrot Diamond*, in October 1985, her singing career has taken off, and her former life as a teacher has been replaced by a musician's life of songwriting, touring and fitting in a busy performance schedule.

But the fishing life remains part of who she is, as Charlotte wrote in a statement for the Richmond Museum's Heritage of Faith: Spiritual and Sacred Places exhibit, in 2005.

◀ Charlotte Diamond, in the CBC Radio One Vancouver studio for taping of "Healing the Heart."

"We became part of a wonderful community of fishermen and families. Although Harry left fishing in 1991 to help manage my music business, we have remained connected with friends who still fish or work in the fishing industry. Fishing is dangerous work and often a lonely occupation so far away from home. We remember those fishermen lost at sea and friends from Steveston and other ports who are no longer with us."

So she and Harry go to the Fishermen's Memorial to walk and reflect beside the sea, and they go back for remembrance. "Every time I go out there, it's a place to touch back in history. I think of all those looking out and then coming back to safe harbour," Charlotte said thoughtfully.

Walking in this area along the dikes, on Garry Point and Scotch Pond, Charlotte is "filled with a feeling of spaciousness, openness, after the noisy, crowded cities. It's nice to find a spot to get your mind clear. We're often afraid of solitude because it brings deep emotions, but we don't need to be afraid. But the emotions often move us to do what we need to do. A lot of good writing comes out of despair and anger."

Both Charlotte and Harry told me how they mourn the demise of the West Coast fishery, so for them, the feeling of loss at the memorial is not just for those who have died, but also for a way of life. When Charlotte touches the memorial and feels the cool, bronze bas-relief beneath her hands, she feels a reverence for the sea life of the fisherman and a mourning for the "abundant silver fish that we don't have anymore; a mourning for an industry that was a community on the sea, that we may lose; a deep sense of loss of something special that helped form my family—my boys loved the sea."

Many others in BC, with its long and proud fishing history, may feel a similar sense of mourning, and pride, but may not have a place that allows them to reflect on those conflicting feelings. The Fishermen's Memorial, just beside the river, shaped like a fishing-net needle and located in an open, visible place for all to see, is a site where the complexity of feelings can be honoured and understood.

"But," Charlotte went on to say, "you lift your eyes and look out to the water, the sunset and the future on the other side. You get to have both

▶ Rick Hansen fishing on the Fraser River. COURTESY OF THE RICK HANSEN
MAN IN MOTION FOUNDATION

sensations. We mourn what has passed, but then we are resilient, a true test of our humanity."

Charlotte's music often focuses on the sea, or water themes, and she frequently writes songs when she is out walking. "I need to be outdoors. I write the rhythm in my head. At Garry Point and on the dykes, it is always inspiring." She also has a place on Sechelt Inlet, where she loves to go for long swims, immersed in the sea. "Obviously, I have been really influenced by water and living here."

→>-<←

A NOTHER BRITISH COLUMBIAN who feels that way is "Man In Motion" Rick Hansen, president and CEO of the Rick Hansen Foundation. The mighty Fraser River is the body of water that has most influenced his life; like sacred rivers around the world, it became a part of his healing.

Rick, now a Companion of the Order of Canada, whose foundation has raised over $200 million for spinal cord research, was paralyzed from the waist down in a car accident coming back from a fishing trip when he was 15 years old. Part of his therapy was to get back on the water and go fishing, and that, he said "played a pivotal role in my rehabilitation after my injury. It helped me regain my confidence in life and made me realize I was still the same person—the outdoorsman, the athlete, the adventurer. Fishing taught me that I didn't need the use of my legs in order to be whole; it helped me see that I could still set goals and dreams, and gave me a great sense of belief and hope for my future."

The Fraser River remains Rick's sacred place even today, as he expressed persuasively during the Heritage of Faith exhibit in Richmond.

"The Fraser River is a place I hold close to my heart. Some of my fondest childhood memories include the hours I spent fishing on its water and shores. The Fraser is the lifeblood of this province; it is a place where I feel connected to nature's overwhelming beauty and diversity. On the Fraser, I become focused on the myriad simple things that contribute to the complexity of life, and while we are small components, we all have an important role to play. My time on the

Fraser is precious to me and inspires and motivates me to ensure that it is preserved for future generations. It is an honour to pay tribute to and to work to protect this sacred place."

Rick does just that through his work as chair of the Fraser River Sturgeon Conservation Society and the Pacific Salmon Endowment Fund Society.

"Today, fishing remains a big part of my life. It allows me to take time away from the demands of everyday life and to find focus and clarity. It's also an opportunity for me to give back and to help preserve the natural resource that has

▶ Michael McCarthy at Ogden Point, Victoria.

given me so much joy in life. My favourite times on the Fraser are spent in the company of friends or family. It's a peaceful, relaxing time to reconnect with each other and with the environment."

➼➤➤⦁➤

WE SEEM TO understand intuitively the importance and symbolism of immersing ourselves in water. The cleansing. The baptism. The return to something elemental. When I asked CBC radio host Shelagh Rogers of *Sounds Like Canada* to tell me about the place she feels is sacred, I was quite moved by her response.

"Strangely, my sacred place is Locarno Beach in Vancouver. I say strangely because it isn't very secluded and in the summer it is positively ripping with people. But for me [in the fall], especially, I love going to the beach and slipping into the water. I wear a wetsuit, so I can do this all year long and it is especially restorative in fall and winter because there are so few people around. I love being weightless in the water … I love splashing around like a kid. I love just floating and staring at the mountains or the sky. Once or twice, a seal has come to join me and that was a profound thrill. It's like swimming in the biggest pool of them all. I always emerge feeling serene and purified, and reborn from the water."

➼➤➤⦁➤

THE HEALING QUALITIES of water, physical, spiritual and emotional, were also clear to Michael McCarthy after he suffered a head injury in a serious car accident in 2006. Michael is Nuu-chah-nulth, from the Ucluelet First Nation, and a communications consultant who lives in Victoria. After his accident, Michael could barely walk, so the first body of water he turned to was his hot tub, where he would immerse himself to soak and meditate up to six times a day. It may sound a little odd to think of a hot tub as a sacred bath, but Michael believes that as he sat in the water quietly meditating, his cells began to remember what they

needed to do, and his mind could start healing. "I could easily have stayed paralyzed from my injuries, but the chemistry of the body allowed the long-term effects to go away. I'm becoming more of who I am [since the accident]."

The Nuu-chah-nulth word *oos-umch* means to bathe and pray, and refers, Michael said, to the "deepest connection you can create to nature" by immersing yourself in water—the sea, a river or, in this case, even a hot tub. Michael found that by submerging himself, he also tapped into the "ancestral, cultural knowledge that Granny taught me. There's an ocean inside us. We are a body of water, and that's why it's so natural to be around water. We respond to the moon."

Michael loves the sea along Dallas Road in Victoria—how it sounds and smells and moves—and often goes to the beaches there. He is a bit of a Renaissance man: he plays the flute (has released a CD), has written a book of romantic poetry and likes scholarly research. He has spoken at Royal Roads University on the blending of ancestral teachings and university learning, is a businessman interested in water sustainability issues, and misses his Native language when he's away from Nuu-chah-nulth territory. I asked him what is sacred. His answer: "Granny said you have to tell stories."

► Heather Botting-O'Brien at pond at University of Victoria.

Michael's manner is calm, centred, attentive. He listens to people, so no doubt he hears the teachings his granny taught him. He remembers going to potlatches with her as a child, eating, sitting, being quiet with her. He knows that his route to healing is through his family, most especially his wife. And he also knows his "healing will always involve water. There's no closer place to be in touch with nature."

-+->-<-+-

THE OCEAN, vast, deep, and mysterious, with its daily ebb and flow, is, according to Heather Botting-O'Brien, a feminine symbol that draws people to the West Coast. She believes the popularity of pagan beliefs on the coast is due to several things—"We're notorious for being more liberal than the east, more accepting, more laid back"—but also to our proximity to water.

"I think the ocean has a lot to do with it. It's a powerful symbol of the goddess and fertility ... I think there's tremendous energy from the ocean that permeates life here."

We live on the "ring of fire" and she thinks it's no coincidence that the Shinto and Tao beliefs of Japan, across the water on the other rim of the Pacific, also focus on the flow of water. The ceremonies carried out by the Wiccan group at the University of Victoria are often held at the little pond adjacent to the Interfaith Chapel. The shoreline, or edge of the pond, has been the location for well over 100 Wiccan rituals, so this area has become a particularly sacred spot for Heather.

The place that Beverley Sinclair, former editor of the *Georgia Straight* newspaper in Vancouver and now coordinator of the Kwantlen College journalism program, chose as her sacred place is one of the best loved of West Coast destinations.

"For me, it's the beaches in the Long Beach area near Tofino. The patterns the waves leave on the sand, the wildness of the water and the weather, and the constant sound of those crashing waves, even when I'm sleeping, just does something to me. I go there at least once a year and vow to go more."

Sombrio Beach is a place I need to go to more often. In fact, I've said to Russ, "Take me there whenever life gets too wound up, when you know I need to slow down and feel peaceful." Even so, we don't get there nearly enough.

Sombrio, on the west coast of Vancouver Island on the way to Port Renfrew, has a spiritual presence for me, more than other beaches, and I'm not sure why. Maybe it's the ancient trees that line the path to the beach. I was sad to see one of them, a huge old Sitka spruce, now sprawled across the trail, perhaps a victim of winter's wild windstorms.

On the beach, the waves lap as rhythmically as a heartbeat, and ethereal fog rolls in and out most days of the year. I've returned to Sombrio many times for rituals and feasts, to remember the dead and to celebrate the living. We commemorated the life of the cherished BC poet and writer, Rona Murray, our friend, by climbing a large boulder, reading selections from one of Rona's books and scattering flowers on the waves below.

→>-<-

I INVITED FRIENDS to join me at Sombrio for my birthday one year. We spread out a banquet on the smooth rocks, barbecued salmon on cedar sticks over an open fire, Kwagiulth style, and boiled huge Quadra Island prawns in the salt water for an exquisite, gourmet West Coast feast.

After dinner we built a campfire of driftwood and sat around it. Two guitars were brought out and we sang, listened, laughed, sat. It was an evening in late June, one of the longest days of the year. Slowly, twilight smudged the scene, the sea faded to black and darkness enfolded us. Life felt simple and complete. I snuggled in the sand, leaning against a log, and felt warmth, within and without. I tilted my head back and saw a shooting star. I could hear the in-and-out lapping of the waves, and knew I would sleep well.

I 7

Gardens Private and Public

*If we could see the miracle of a single flower clearly,
our whole life would change.*

From the teachings of Buddha in
Buddha's Little Instruction Book,
by JACK KORNFIELD

DRIVING SLOWLY down the road, I peered at street numbers and looked for the home of poets Lorna Crozier and Patrick Lane, whose garden became famous after the publication of Patrick's *There Is a Season: A Memoir*. Suddenly, there was the house, set back from the road with an explosion of purple wisteria climbing up beside the front door, winding past the second floor and right onto the roof: heady, fanciful, profuse, a sort of floral Rorschach covering most of the front of the house.

As I approached the front steps, mesmerized by the sprawling grandeur of the drooping blooms and thinking how this explains Patrick's many poems about wisteria, I heard a sonorous baritone, "I'm here, in the garden." A rich voice, perfect for reading poetry or soothing a wild beast.

I was there that day because my friends Dave and Lesley Preston, avid gardeners themselves, had given me *There Is a Season* for my birthday and written

in it the inscription, "We thought you might like to read about Patrick Lane's Sacred Place." Of course, they meant his garden, which is not only the setting for his book, but the spot where, at long last, the well-known poet-turned-prose-writer allowed himself to heal after a lifetime of addictions and ghosts. Reading Patrick's book is a stroll through his metaphors and memories, at times a ramble through poetic imagery, at times an abrupt halt beside the raw clarity of his reminiscences. If ever there were a voice raised in praise of a sacred place, it is Patrick's ode to his garden.

We sat under a tree on the lawn, across from the dry pond (made up of rocks and borders and a vaguely native rock carving), and surrounded by flowers and plants. I was aware that I had been generously welcomed into a sanctuary.

"For me, it's the most private of places. I've never opened it up to anyone," Patrick said, admitting that he had even turned down requests from the local garden club. He didn't want his refuge to become a tourist attraction.

"Ninety-five percent of the time, it's just Lorna and me and the two cats." One of them, the deliciously named Basho (after the 17th-century Japanese poet-pilgrim), as if to prove him right, appears and stretches out majestically in front of us.

Throughout the ages, sacred places have often been kept secret. It's a conundrum, in fact, that is a common problem for the First Nations of British

◀ Patrick Lane and Basho in the garden.

Columbia, who are often reluctant to reveal the exact locations of sites they wish to protect. It is not hard to understand the desire to keep sacred secrets.

Yet, Patrick warmly received me and was graciously willing, in fact, seemed pleased, to talk about this tenth of a hectacre that "really is a sacred place. It's a small paradise.

"I get a kind of a blessing, particularly in the night. There is nothing more exquisite than a moonlit garden. I can find peace here, contentment here, where I don't have to create fictions. It's a real place, not created out of language, a non-verbal world."

For a poet and weaver of words, the tangible presence of earth and mosses, of star magnolia delicately white in spring and tulip petals glowing at twilight, of the pond with carp (at least the ones that escape the heron's swoops) nestled among the plants, is "a place of utter transformation."

"It's an intimate paradise of my own, and it transcends life and death."

And it's been a way to reorder, to rearrange his world, to have some control over a chaotic life of addiction and wandering. Writing about his garden was his therapy, and because Patrick is a two-fingered typist, the very act of typing slowed him down. "This garden did heal me. The first year of my sobriety, this was my sanctuary, the holiest place, the ark of the covenant for me."

Patrick and Lorna have now moved on to an "exquisitely designed" house with sliding doors leading out to a Japanese garden, very quiet, not far from their old home. And they love the new place too. I was surprised when I heard they had moved: they had seemed so rooted in the old. When I asked Patrick how it felt to leave the garden that had helped him heal, that had even attained a certain level of fame when *There Is a Season* was published, he told me the new garden has reinvigorated him.

"Gardens come and go; they move on to be tended by others." And he said that after he wrote his memoir, the old place "became a kind of fiction—it became a book."

The garden, a sacred, healing place, was the setting for his Shakespearean monologue, scripted carefully each day for a whole year, a vessel holding the

be a Japanese and a Canadian as well. It's assisting me in transforming to be whatever I feel comfortable being."

When Tomoko left Japan with her Japanese-Canadian husband, Dennis, in early April 1974, she didn't realize the effect her departure had on her father. For days afterwards, he would leave his house each evening and walk to a cherry tree growing in a nearby schoolyard. He stood under the tree, blossoms scattered at his feet, and cried with the anguish only a parent can know: his only daughter Tomoko was gone.

Tomoko didn't know of her father's tears and found out about his nightly vigil only when her mother told her years later. But as a homesick young wife in a strange culture, missing the familiar blossoms of home, she shed tears of her own. Then one day, squeezed into a crowded bus in Vancouver, she glanced out the window and spotted a cherry tree in full bloom, the street beneath it covered with the familiar pink petals.

"From that moment, I related my life to Canada and [planted] my feet on Canadian soil." And she began to embrace the bicultural nature of her life. Today, she feels more at home in Canada, with her husband and two Canadian-born daughters, than in Japan, and said, "I think one of the gains [here] is I understand more of myself, and in a way the cherry blossoms helped me." Seeing the annual spring display gives Tomoko a chance for self-reflection.

Over a thousand cherry trees from Japan, purchased thanks to a gift from the city's vibrant Japanese community, were planted on the streets of Victoria more than 65 years ago. For Tomoko, it is a tradition to enjoy the trees each spring, touching the bark, smelling the blossoms and listening to the tree.

"I think I can forget anything I don't want to hear there," and in those moments, she becomes immersed in a dialogue between the tree and herself, a meditation on the duality of nature: yin and yang, shadow and sunlight.

"I'm not religious," Tomoko said, but she acknowledged that she feels a kinship with Buddhism and Shintoism. The Shinto shrines always have cherry trees, and "seek spirituality from Nature": perhaps the cherry blossoms play a part. "It's a kind of superpower I feel: wherever life goes, always spring is coming.

► Tomoko and her hanami in spring.

Cherry blossoms for me always assure [me] that happiness and spring will come."

For many years, Tomoko has worked to bring this sense of hope and connection to immigrant women like herself, living on the West Coast. "I think [for] many immigrant women, it's challenging to find a place to feel comfortable, to feel herself." She almost single-handedly started the Immigrant Women's Group of the Cowichan Valley Intercultural and Immigrant Aid Society in Duncan back in the 1980s. When she went to school each day to pick up her daughters, she would look for other immigrant women-standing shyly doing the same. She would in-troduce herself and invite them to join the group; many are still friends 25 years later.

Later, Tomoko worked with women's groups, immigrant families and refugees at Victoria's Intercultural Association. She's now working part-time at the UVic Intercultural Student Family Services, and she'll probably go on working to improve the lives of immigrant women and their families in some capacity pretty much forever.

In her active, service-oriented life, the ritual of hanami is a welcome time of silence and a link to her childhood, "both hopeful and nostalgic." She remembers going with her family every year to spread a blanket under a cherry tree and share a sushi picnic, a rite of spring that is widespread in Japan even today. After the blossoms have faded and the leaves come out, they are cooked, salted and used in a special cookie called *sakura mochi* (cherry dessert). On March 3, Girls' Day in Japan, the sakura mochi, made from leaves preserved the previous spring, is served, only to girls, in an honouring of womanhood that to this day makes Tomoko feel both optimistic and melancholy.

Every spring she receives a package from her cousin in Japan, and drinks cherry blossom tea. This feminine symbolism seems appropriate too, as she has spent so much of her life working on women's issues and trying to integrate immigrant women more fully into Canadian society.

For Tomoko, the gentle cherry blossoms are a symbol of both life and death, "the point of past and future" and an integral part of how she can renew and transform herself—and now, a sacred place as well.

Gardens of any type are where many of us renew our connection to the Earth, meditate on our lives and find time to delight in beauty; they remind us that we, like the flowers, can be fragile or resilient, depending on the season.

18

The Unexpected

-+>-+>-<+-<+-

*The real voyage of discovery consists not in seeking new landscapes
but in having new eyes.*

MARCEL PROUST, French novelist

-+>-<+-

WILLIAM HEAD INSTITUTION, a minimum security prison, is a place where, despite the harshness and cynicism of lives gone awry, healing and spiritual growth take place. A Buddhist lama, Margaret Ludwig, urged me to go to the Buddhist Sacred Meditation Garden there, a garden that she had worked with inmates to create. She firmly believed it should be included in anyone's accounting of the sacred in our area. Garry, an inmate (or as he preferred to say, prisoner) walked down each day to care for the garden, beside the Pacific Ocean, and to observe the gulls, eagles and herons. It was there that he felt a peacefulness he hadn't experienced for years.

On the small promontory of land where the garden sits, arbutus trees grow beside carefully placed cherry trees, two simple cedar benches and statues of the Buddha occupy a grassy meditation area and deep blue camas and delicate shooting stars bloom each spring.

"When you're in that spot, you're alive," Garry said. He brought tea, the steaming pot swathed in towels to keep the contents warm in the chill morning air, and offered his homemade brownies, double chocolate with dates. "This is a wonderful, wonderful spot," he continued, as we sat and sipped the tea. "I've been in a lot of penitentiaries, you know. To me, it's been the most therapeutic thing, this relationship with the ocean … I'm not in prison when I'm down here. It's helped heal me." A convicted drug dealer, who served nearly 20 years in the US and Canada, Garry had found his sacred place. The spot officially became a meditation garden in 1992 and has since been blessed by three Buddhist lamas from India as "an energy place for peace."

Garry and I were accompanied that day by Chris Trehearne, the affable groundskeeper and horticulture instructor at William Head, who also seemed to feel the spell of that tranquil spot.

"There's an incredible sense of peace when I walked down there, looking out over the waves. Serenity has taken over the spot," said Chris, a long-time employee who has seen many changes at the prison over the years. Later, he gave me a tour of the grounds, including the well-used chapel, the Wiccan stone circle and the Salmon House, where Aboriginal inmates sometimes find a spiritual path.

One of the programs that takes place in the Spiritual (or Big) Room of the Salmon House is the In Search of Your Warrior program, described by manager

◄ The Buddhist Sacred Meditation Garden at William Head Institution.

Wendy Townsend as "an intense Aboriginally focused program that deals with the roots of rage or anger in a culturally sensitive way."

CBC radio host Jo-Ann Roberts and I were invited to sit in on a talking circle held by recent graduates of the Warrior program. Talking circles are always moving—a time for people to share their truths in a safe and secure environment—and I had taken part in many during my years of teaching at Hiiye'yu Lelum, the Native Friendship Centre in Duncan. But it was quite different to hear prison inmates talk openly and frankly about their lives, their crimes, their brokenness and healing, with Jo-Ann and me, people they had just met.

Not only that, the men knew ahead of time that their stories might wind up on national radio. Yet every man there chose to tell his story, no matter how serious his crime or how difficult his life. The level of trust in the room was startling, and the degree of comfort the men felt within those walls could be at least partly attributed to the sacred space they had created.

Wendy, who has overseen many programs there, said, "I feel very strongly about that building as well. I find when I go there, I have all the time in the world. It's easy to talk in that room. A very special place. I see the response of inmates who go to ceremonies there. Having a building and a place to go where they can share in a circle has a huge impact, even on the staff."

Both the interior and the exterior of the Salmon House are beautifully decorated with Native art and totem poles. The Spiritual Room was built in the style of a ceremony room of a First Nations longhouse. We started by sharing coffee and doughnuts at a long table; then chairs were set up in the traditional circle formation and we were all asked to take our seats.

We removed our jewellery, watches and glasses. The smudge ceremony, during which cleansing smoke from a small pile of smouldering sweetgrass is waved over each person, who then "washes" it over his or her face and arms and torso, comes first. In a talking circle, a talking stick or other object, such as the eagle's feather we used that day, is chosen and the person holding the feather has permission to talk. Normally, no one else speaks until they are given the feather. One by one, the men talked about their crimes, their inability to function in

various ways and their desire to transform their lives, starting here, within this sacred space.

"In every institution across Canada, there should be a facility like this," said Daniel, a program participant serving time for dangerous driving. "It helps us retain our lost culture. Our lost heritage. Instead of being saddened by being stuck with the label of Indian, you can be proud of your heritage."

Other men talked about the profound changes in their lives, thanks to the program held within the Salmon House walls. Alan, serving five years for manslaughter, said, "Having the Salmon House and Native grounds here is very important. I don't know what would have happened; I was an angry person, until I went to this In Search of Your Warrior program. It's absolutely amazing. They give us tools … and how to heal, the sweats, the ceremonies. I finally found where I belonged."

The idyllic setting of William Head Institution, referred to by some as "Club Fed," is unusually scenic for a prison, and local taxpayers often complain about that, but more than one inmate has told me that this natural setting next to the ocean has helped him heal.

→>-<←

A DIFFERENT seaside setting, across the water in Vancouver, is the backdrop for the Vancouver Folk Music Festival, a gala celebration held each summer,

◄ Talking circle in Salmon House.

with thousands of people listening to dozens of musicians. Jericho Park, where the folk fest is held, is right on English Bay, with the mountains of the north shore etched in the distance and the lights of the city twinkling at night. It's a joyful, festive event, and for freelance travel journalist Angela Murrills, it is also her sacred place.

"An ideal community" for one weekend, is how Angela explained it. "It's like this is how the world should be: people wearing gaily coloured clothes, happy, getting up and dancing … and the whole world is represented. A sense of community. This is what heaven should be like. It's even got the good food!"

Angela has taken her daughter, now in her 20s, to the festival since she was little, and loved the feeling that children were "completely safe" there. The sea of blankets and tarps people put down each year in front of the main stage to claim their spots for the evening concerts reminds Angela of "little homesteads" that people set up. She feels crime is unlikely in that huge crowd. The world-music groups she has heard over the years inevitably led to "that kind of magical thing that happens when you discover a culture that's not your own. And all these interesting things for children, who are often not part of things."

The setting at Jericho Beach is, in Angela's opinion, "wonderful to wander through, or go blackberry picking, see people sleeping among the trees—it's harmony, in all senses of the world—a little microcosm that you wish could extend to the country at large."

It would be hard to find a more picturesque concert setting in the world. One evening as I left the folk fest, the sky was a brilliant pink, and a warm golden sliver of light shone on the boats in the bay, so glorious that people walked to the beach to stare. The music floated out over the water, and sure enough, there were people dancing in front of the stage. Yes, I could imagine a heaven like that.

-+>-<+-

Not far from Jericho Beach, however, Vancouver's Downtown Eastside is a place that doesn't leap to mind when you mention the word "sacred." We

► Leslie Alexander, now a musician with three CDs released. PHOTO BY ERIC MILNER

hear about the poverty, addictions, crime, homelessness and hopelessness there. It's a pretty bleak picture.

Until Leslie Alexander tells her story. She arrived in Vancouver "at loose ends, a happy chick, flat broke, with no ambitions." But she could sing and play the guitar. Fast forward: within a few years, she'd become an alcoholic, struggling with drug addiction, busking on the street for coins. "A mess" is how she described it. But even then, she felt a sense of kinship with her neighbours and was "intensely grateful for the acceptance I was offered there, expressed through gestures such as a shared cigarette, or a smile—it was a true neighbourhood."

Life started to improve a little, as people offered to help her out, and Leslie made up her mind to get off booze and drugs. One Saturday night, in the midst of her personal struggle, she said to herself, "I need a sign" that things will be okay, and headed out, wandering the streets. She walked past St. Paul's Parish Church on Cordova Street and was curious to see lights on at 10:30 PM. She slipped inside, saw a group of people holding candles and realized it was the Easter Vigil mass. Someone handed her a candle, and she stood peacefully in the group, thinking, "Well, maybe this is my sign." Suddenly, the flame from another candle accidentally set her hair on fire, and the next thing Leslie knew, people were slapping her head, putting out the flames. She sat there afterwards, stunned. The Irish priest, Father Bob, came over and sat beside her, his eyes twinkling, and said, "I just want you to know, not everything is a sign." He became her mentor and friend, and a couple of years later married her to her music producer. Today, Leslie is sober, has released three CDs and has a successful musical career. But even now, when she needs inspiration, she goes back to the neighbourhood she considers her sacred place.

"Like many others, I was able to improve my sense of self-worth while living there as a direct result of kindnesses given by other residents, particularly those who lived at the Ford Building at the corner of Main and Hastings, and at St. Paul's Church on Cordova. Many people go to the Downtown Eastside expecting to die there and instead are reborn, as I was.

"There's a lot of hope in the Downtown Eastside. You find it in the strangest places. In my own experience, you don't really need hope unless you've gone to the dark. There's tremendous potential for people that are at the absolute worst stages of their lives. 'Cause once you go to that dark place, if you can flip to the other side, you have so much more light to give, and I've seen it many many times down there, many times.

"I believe that the broken ones in our society have a special function in the well of life—they are here to awaken our humanity and compassion, to pull us out of our natural self-centredness and ask, how can I be of service here? How can I help the healing process? In so doing, we save our own souls."

-➤->-<-←-

"WHERE IS YOUR sacred place?" I asked Dr. Basil Boulton, a councillor for the Township of Esquimalt.

"When I'm with my patients," he replied without hesitation. His answer surprised and delighted me. Basil is a pediatrician, and it is easy to picture him talking to, caring for and sometimes saving the life of a child within that sacred space. Or, by contrast, experiencing profound sorrow when he loses a young patient.

Basil practised medicine in Victoria for 35 years, yet remembers almost every

◄ Basil Boulton remembers each patient.

patient. He talked about "Joey" or "Susan" (but not for print), and said, "I have to give you names because that's how I think of my kids. Not 'a kid with cerebral palsy.'" He talked about cases that turned out well and those with tragic endings, each story told with a freshness and immediacy that made it seem like it happened last week. "Every relationship with a patient" was, for Basil, a sacred place.

He treated the usual pediatric cases and the tougher ones: fetal alcohol syndrome, child abuse, terminal illness. Along the way, he built lasting relationships with his "kids" and their families, and watched his patients grow up. Reflecting on hundreds and hundreds of hospital visits and office appointments, he said, "I found myself in a sacred place in being able to touch and impact the lives of so many people. It's all expressed through particular children and ... when that child was in front of you ... they were the most special person in the world, my favourite patient. Whenever somebody came, you had to find out what their special need or ability was, and deal with that, and it varied so much. The children for whom you could do the most were the children with cancer. Maybe you couldn't give them the medicine, but you could give them a piece of yourself."

For Basil, it is the specific circumstances of relationship and ritual that make a place sacred. For others too, geographical location is not always relevant when they choose their sacred places. One person told me she finds her sacred place in heartfelt conversations with people who come to see her at times of personal crisis. And some people believe you can create a sacred space simply by drawing a circle around yourself.

Sacred places can be situational, delineated by circumstances. Most often, a place is considered sacred because of its inherent hallowedness, a quality we connect to a specific, permanent location. But sacredness can also be experienced through the intentions, rituals and attitudes we bring to a spot, a temporary sanctification that can occur almost anywhere. Sacred places include both the exterior landscape around us and the interior landscape of our hearts.

[*Author's note: Basil Boulton died suddenly in January, 2008. Hundreds attended his memorial service, including many former patients and their families.*]

19

Remembrance:
Standing on the Threshold

->->->-<-<-

Oh, there will come a day, a twilight,
When I shall sink to rest
In deep wet moss and cool blue shadows
Upon a mountain's breast.

LEW SARETT, in
Life Prayers from Around the World

->-<-

PLACES OF remembrance can be consoling, horrifying, contemplative or tranquil, but they provide us with a profound connection to our mortality and to that which is beyond our knowing. For some, to eternity. These are places that link us to those who have gone before us, peacefully or tragically. They are the liminal places, where we sometimes feel close to the next reality, however we may envision it.

There is an undeniable sacredness in places where great pain or suffering has occurred, like Ground Zero, site of the former World Trade Center in New York City, World War II concentration camps or the abandoned villages of Haida Gwaii where hundreds of Haida ancestors died of smallpox. People go to these places partly to touch the depths of shared sorrow that defines our humanity.

We go to places of remembrance for other reasons, too. To honour. To learn. To find strength. These are the things that draw author Evelyn C. White to the sacred place she has found on Salt Spring Island. Her "most treasured place" is

◀ For Evelyn White, the gravesite of Sylvia Stark is a place of inspiration.

the gravesite of Sylvia Stark, one of the original Salt Spring pioneers. Evelyn invited me to come over and visit the site with her.

I was delighted by her invitation, partly because the older I get the more I believe in synchronicity (which I think would be satisfying to Carl Jung and to others on a pilgrimage of any sort). But it does seem more than coincidence that Evelyn and I have the same name. I was born Evelyn Star Weiss, always called Star. "Weiss" means "white" in German. So, there you have it: Evelyn White, writer and former newspaper reporter born in the US and living in BC, meet Evelyn White, writer and former newspaper reporter born in the US and living in BC. But we don't look at all alike. When I first met Evelyn, she was gleefully getting dreadlocks twisted into her long hair, and had probably located one of the few people in Victoria who knew how to do it.

A few weeks later, we visited Sylvia Stark's grave in Central Cemetery, where we sat on lawn chairs at the foot of the grave, facing the headstone. It felt a little like we were joining Sylvia for a neighbourly chat.

"I think this is the greatest thing, that Sylvia and all these other black pioneers are here," Evelyn said. "The movement from slavery to liberation is right here. She came here to be free. I came here free. I can choose how to shape my years."

And the choice Evelyn made was to settle on Salt Spring, just as Sylvia Stark and her family did nearly 150 years ago. By spending time at the gravesite of this pioneering woman, a former slave who lived to the grand age of 105, Evelyn feels refreshed and renewed, grateful "to be a witness for so much of our history." For her, this site memorializes the courage and tenacity of the black ancestors.

Being a witness to African-American history has been a lifetime pursuit for

Evelyn, a former reporter for the *San Francisco Chronicle* and advisory board member of *Ms* magazine. She spent 10 years researching and writing the first authorized biography of Alice Walker, Pulitzer Prize–winning author of *The Color Purple* and a woman who has been a literary pioneer making history for decades. Now that *Alice Walker: a Life* is in print and even in paperback, Evelyn has deliberately chosen to move from the US to the quieter life of Salt Spring, an island she is drawn to because of its long history of black settlement.

The matriarch of those settlers was Sylvia Stark, who would no doubt smile to see that she now appears on the Salt Spring five-dollar bill, a locally accepted currency. Sylvia Estes Stark was born a slave in Missouri in 1839, managed to teach herself to read and write in a time when that was forbidden to slaves, arrived as a free woman on Salt Spring in 1860 and helped her husband carve out a farm in the West Coast wilderness while raising her growing family.

She was part of the group of black settlers who moved to Salt Spring from California at the invitation of James Douglas, governor of the Colony of Vancouver Island, and himself of Guyanese and Scottish descent. One of Sylvia's accomplishments during her long life on Salt Spring was to plant an apple orchard, which continues to bear fruit today on land still owned by Stark family descendants. On the day we visited the cemetery, Evelyn brought an apple and placed it on Sylvia's grave in recognition of this enduring legacy.

For many of us, it is crucial to commemorate the final resting place of those we admire or love, to sanctify the spot that is the threshold between life, death or the next world. Evelyn's visits to Sylvia Stark's gravesite echo Alice Walker's search for the burial site of African-American novelist Zora Neale Hurston. Alice wanted to pay tribute to her forebear, and Evelyn is on a parallel pilgrimage: honouring and remembering the life of a pioneer black woman who broke new ground, literally, on this West Coast island.

"I'm grateful for having that model in front of me, [and feel] enormous gratitude for being witness to the scope of the story," Evelyn said. "I'm mindful that people like Sylvia Stark were forbidden to learn to read and write because of the force of words."

▶ Myra Falls at our arrival.

→>‹←

W<small>E ALL HAVE</small> ways to bear witness, and they often involve place. Our honouring can be as simple and poignant as erecting a roadside shrine at the site of an accident or as textured as the transformation that eases us from life to death to remembering, from hospice to cremation to the scattering of ashes.

Photographer Peter Paul Harnisch, who stopped to photograph roadside memorials along desolate BC roads for years, said he felt powerfully drawn to these spontaneous shrines: a time to sit and think about lives lost, about the loud, horrific event that occurred at that spot, but also to feel a "real sense of calm and peace." Maybe Peter was tapping into our collective need for remembrance.

→>‹←

M<small>Y NEED TO</small> remember person and place brings me to the next story: the final chapter in the life of my friend Sharon Hall. Sharon carried the image of Myra Falls within her until she died, many months later, in another place that had become sacred to her, the Victoria Hospice. A few weeks before her death, she and I went out to coffee with a former classmate of hers, and his wife and little boy. Sharon was happy, pleased to see Tim's photographs, laughing at the antics of his toddler.

On the way to her apartment afterwards, when Tim and his family had gone, Sharon turned to me and said she knew she didn't have much time left, that she could feel things falling apart within her. And then she said, "But that's okay. I'll die and your grandchild will be born." The cycle would go on. I didn't know it then, but as she spoke, my daughter had started labour. My first grandchild, beautiful little Sophia Emily Broadland, was born the next day.

Sharon was proud of the fact that she survived for months longer than her oncologist had predicted. I think she felt a certain smug satisfaction in defying the medical prediction. And she enjoyed life to the last taste. Just a few days before she passed away in the wonderfully supportive milieu of the Victoria Hospice,

I arrived at her room with watermelon, a favourite of hers, and she quickly wolfed down several pieces with obvious enjoyment and gusto.

I had walked into the hospice that day with the uncut mini watermelon in hand, wondering how I was going to serve it, and was sent to a kitchen area where several volunteers hovered, chatting quietly. Those women went to work, even suggesting the best way to cut the watermelon (across the grain, which I'd never done) and arranging the juicy pink slices on a china plate. As I was about to carry the treat to Sharon's room, one said, "Wait!" and found a flower to place in the middle of the artfully arranged platter. The melon looked mouth-wateringly tempting. I went off gratefully, warmed by this small example of the thoughtful actions, the intentions that make this place what it is. It merely reinforced the Victoria Hospice's reputation as one of the best around; in fact, other hospices call on its staff for guidance.

In her room that day, which turned out to be our last visit, Sharon told me that the hospice had also become a sacred place to her because she felt a freedom there that allowed her to do what she wanted, and people there who would help her to do it. For the past several months, Sharon had been coming into the hospice for respite care, or what she called her "recharging."

There is a bed set aside for the terminally ill who come in for periods of time, a complete rest for them and for their caregivers, so they can go back to their lives at home feeling better for as long as possible. After each respite visit, Sharon would make arrangements for the next one: "I'll be back in April for a week."

Knowing that this care existed helped her live longer, I'm convinced. Getting this care was a lifeline. Compassion lives here, in the spiritually charged

◀ The rainbow appeared above the falls.

atmosphere where the veil between life and death is exquisitely thin. When people do cross over, they know they are enfolded within the grace and gentleness of a sacred place.

There are many gifts we can receive from those who know their time here is limited. From Sharon I learned about acceptance and the courage to face fears, how to live out your life with the appreciation for each day that we all mean to feel, sometime. Sharon was flattered when the staff asked if they could tell her story about how much the hospice meant to her, in their fundraising letter for 2007. When a donation of $10,000 came into the hospice just after the letter went out, Sharon was thrilled, pleased that she could help leave this legacy.

One day when I went in to visit her, a man was perched on the arm of a chair beside her, chatting amiably, continuing on for a few minutes when I sat down, then moving on to let me visit with her. I thought he must be a volunteer: it turned out, to my surprise, that he was her doctor. He wasn't standing stethoscope in hand, talking doctor-ese. He was leaning over sociably, arms folded across his chest, in no hurry, talking about something non-medical, as I recall. He was simply a friendly visitor.

When Sharon died, she had one last request. Would I go back to Myra Falls and spread her ashes at her favourite spot on Earth, the place we had journeyed to together almost two years earlier? Of course I would. Through that experience, Sharon gave me a final gift too. I was able to face my own fears of the unknown, of the rituals of death, of how one does this, of suitably living up to an occasion of this importance.

Russ and I planned the trip for a Sunday afternoon, rain or shine, but we were dismayed when, not far from our goal, it began to pour. Well, we'd brought a large umbrella and hiking boots, and were prepared to persevere. But as we approached the falls, the sun began to filter tentatively through the clouds, and by the time we hiked out onto the rocks, full sunlight sparkled on the cascading water. No one else was there at that moment, though we had seen visitors leaving just as we arrived and more people arrived shortly after our ceremony. It seemed right to be alone. I had chosen a couple of selections to read beside the water.

And I will flow back
Into the lifestream
To think like a mountain
And sing like a river.

Mary de La Valette

And yield a body ... bruised with earthly scars,
To the cool oblivion of evening,
Of solitude and stars.

Lew Sarett

Russ gently immersed the bag of ashes in the water, and they were carried into the current. We knew a part of Sharon would be there, under the stars that night, soon to be swept away down into Buttle Lake below.

As we spent time at the falls remembering Sharon, I understood why investigators take people back to the crime scene to jog their memories through the power of place. Being back in the same location, I suddenly remembered details of our earlier trip: I saw the overgrown trail we had started to take to go down to the foot of the falls. When we decided to head back as the trail got too rough for Sharon, she was disappointed, felt unfinished. This time, Russ and I completed the hike to the bottom, a pilgrimage for Sharon. When we came back up and sat once more beside the rocks near where we had spread her ashes, a rainbow appeared just above the lower falls in front of us. It was clear that Sharon was saying goodbye.

As we drove off, a rainstorm moved down the lake, the sky darkened and the rain let loose again. It seemed to both of us that the day had unfolded exactly as it was meant to, tucking us into a pocket of light and warmth and solitude. This return to Sharon's sacred place meant that now it would be a place of remembrance for us as well.

2 0

Home

+>-+>-<+-<+-

I want to remind myself and others that our homes
can become sacred places, filled with life and meaning.
We do not need cathedrals to remind ourselves
to experience the sacred.

Gunilla Norris in *Spiritual Literacy: Reading the Sacred in Everyday Life,*
by FREDERIC and MARY ANN BRUSSAT

+>-<+-

IT'S PREDICTABLE that our homes would and should have elements we consider sacred, yet it's surprising how rarely people say that their home is their sacred place. However, for a few, there was no hesitation: home is the place that tops the list.

I was curious to find out what made them feel this way, and wondered what we could learn from them that might help us more fully appreciate the places where we spend our most intimate, personal times. Are there some homes that are in a location that actually does tap into something intrinsically spiritual and part of the geography of place? That have good feng shui, perhaps?

One house that seems, according to the owners, to fit that category is Maarnada, Maarten and Nadina Schaddelee's oceanside home in Gordon Head, Victoria.

Nadina, a wellness educator, said that on her first visit to the property, "as soon as I walked down the driveway, with my heart almost coming out of my chest, that energy just came through me."

Like when I set foot on Skedans, I couldn't help thinking, even though I still don't quite understand what happened to me there.

Nadina felt an immediate certainty that "we were to live here. Our lives would be changed completely. My whole body was shaking. We were living five minutes from here. It was the house, it was the property: a coming home, a resonance within my soul. This is where my spirit would fly ... I feel you need to go to the [place] that is calling you. This is a sacred site, through intention as well. Some feel it. Some don't. There's something here. This is a dialogue that is of divine nature. For me, on a point of land like this, everything is here, the ocean, land, sky, sunrise, sunset."

◄ Nadina Schaddelee on the Maarnada Rose.

Now, after nearly 30 years living on this land, Nadina believes its particular configuration, jutting out into the sea, holds a "vortex of energy" that she is able to discern.

In anyone's eyes, Maarnada is a stunning spot. A stone walk meanders through the Oriental garden, surrounded by Garry oak, arbutus, yew and fir trees. The dramatically situated point is home to ocean spray, Easter lilies, Oregon grape, Indian plum and native rhododendron. Wild Nootka roses, which Nadina particularly loves, grow along the bank.

The artist's studio, house and property are Maarten's places of inspiration, where his sculptures are displayed in an artistic interweaving with the natural environment. Whales pass by Maarnada frequently, and whales and eagles have become the focus of Maarten's evocative pieces in wood and stone. He and Nadina are affected by the life of the sea every day.

When I was there, Maarten showed me the installation exhibit he was working on. It was the ambitious *Doorways to Spirit* project, a carving of 16 hinged doors, each representing a different faith or spiritual path. Displayed as one hinged circular exhibit, it expresses the idea that we are all headed to the same place, a sacred centre that is mysterious and universal.

The way Maarten sees it, Nadina created the environment there for him to find his gifts. To me, it seems a fortuitous combination of intention and the power of place. And they both say they don't need to leave this sacred spot: it's all there.

-+->-<-+-

KATHERINE GIBSON, author of *Unclutter Your Life* and *Pause*, is also "very reluctant" to leave the sacred space of her home.

"I have created a home, with [husband] Bob that really is our refuge, our oasis of calm, in a very hurried world. And I believe we can create this in any home we choose."

Seated comfortably in her tranquil, mint-green living room, a colour she finds wonderfully soothing, Katherine mused thoughtfully on a subject that is perhaps

more important than ever to her in recent years. After the success of her first book, *Unclutter Your Life* (translated into seven languages), and the flurry of speaking engagements and book publicity that followed, she went through a period of overload, when she realized she needed to simply withdraw for a while, and there was no place better for that than in her own home.

"We need to create an environment that truly reflects where we are on our human journey now. I don't want distractions that pull me into chaos. I have a philosophy that quiet is essential for us to hear our own inner voices, and to hear the voice of God, however we may choose to define it. The world today is so frenetic that it can drown out our own voice and spirit. It's essential to have a place to come to, welcoming, calm, intensely personal, and that's my home. Our homes need to be our sacred places, where we can retreat from the outer world. It gives us the space to contemplate, rest, dream, create; to love, to play, to nourish ourselves spiritually and physically."

On the day I came by for the interview, Katherine insisted we begin the visit with a delicious, leisurely lunch on her patio. I have seen her in her high-speed

◀ Katherine with some of her favourite things, family photos.

public persona, and she is an enthusiastic and energetic presenter and teacher. At home, the pace was purposefully slowed.

"I'm an intensely private person," Katherine admitted, a "closet introvert." She needs her home to be a place of refuge, rather than transformation. "My life outside draws my energy and this gives it back to me. When I choose a home, I try to sense the spirit of the place, and I think places have a feeling. Some homes don't fit, aren't comfortable … and I like small. I like the feeling that the rooms in my home are embracing me."

Katherine and her husband then moved to a home in an older part of Victoria, and were in the process of painting the living room green—still the colour of choice—when I spoke to her and asked what had prompted her move.

"We bring our feelings to a space. We're not *of* a space," Katherine said, a subtle difference that reminded me of Patrick Lane's thoughts when he moved on from his *There Is a Season* garden. Katherine also had yearned for a garden, a place to "play in the dirt, and a wonderful connection with our humanness," and she has a small patch for Zen, woodland and vegetable gardens in her new home.

She loves her new front verandah. Shortly after she moved in, an elderly man came by and told her he used to live in her house 78 years ago. He would sit on that porch and his mother would bring him cookies and milk. That sense of being grounded in a place with good memories also appeals to Katherine.

In this house, Katherine can reach out or retreat within. Like her former home, it has cosy, small rooms ("I think really houses are just substitute wombs") that feel friendly and protective. And she fills them only with things that are beautiful or personally meaningful, that tell a story; she brings in flowers and changes the paintings seasonally.

"What makes a space really sacred are the things in it that speak to you, in a private language," Katherine said.

Heather Botting-O'Brien who, along with her chaplaincy at UVic, is a priestess in the Aquarian Tabernacle Church, understands that feeling. When she looks around in her kitchen, she sees a red terra cotta mask surrounded by beans, which for her is a small altar symbolizing the harvest. The picture of an ancestor beside

◀ The spot where Russ and Star were married.

her bed is another altar, not unlike family pictures placed strategically in most homes.

Heather has five altars (one main altar and one for each direction) in a room in her home set aside for rituals, and several other smaller altars throughout the house. She says Wiccans have altars in their homes as focus points for meditation, and pointed out, "We don't think there's a god in these things. It's not idolatry." She believes that meditating on the symbols around her gives them an energy over time. For Heather and other Wiccans, the most revered sacred spaces are the ones they create within their own homes.

→➤◄←

THE FEELING OF being grounded in a place is what attracts Bruce Lund to his place of sanctuary, the family cabin at Sproat Lake on Vancouver Island.

"Cabins are places of modern-day life that are often the only constant in a person's life. My father built the cabin when I was five and it was a weekender. I spent summers and weekends there and then with my wife and kids, that generation grew up there too. We've all moved, but the cabin has always been there. There's a spiritual serenity."

We've all moved. That is a truth for so many of us. Bruce, though, who has worked in various incarnations for the federal government (and is usually in the middle of a plan to improve services to immigrants, or youth, or First Nations) has held onto his place of memory. It forms a unifying thread in his family's life.

After Labour Day, when the lake is quiet and the air is tangy, Bruce loves to go back to the cabin and sit wrapped up on the porch, with a cup of hot chocolate and a book. One New Year's Eve, his wife, Felicia, suggested they go to the cabin. It was surrounded by a foot of snow when they arrived. They lit a fire, and then stood outside, in "absolute and total silence. Not a thing stirring." It was a way to reconnect to the quiet within, the elemental. "We loved it."

Bruce told me about the laurel bushes his mother planted years ago, the elaborate sundial his brother created so that the shadow of it moves across the cabin during the day, the dinners around the handmade picnic table, the old pump-house they lived in while the family cabin, all 56 square metres of it, was being built. His brother and sister each have a cabin right next door. This is a place of rejuvenation and celebration.

"All these collective memories of my family contribute to a sense of sanctuary and comfort. I'm watching it take root in my kids who are 20-something."

A sense of place, an affinity for a particular piece of land, an emotional attachment that roots us and defines us and links us to our personal history … that's what a cabin or favourite family holiday spot can give us in a world where very few things last a lifetime. As Bruce said, it's often the summer place that represents permanency to a family. Houses can be bought and sold, children move out, but everyone expects to return at some point to the summer cabin.

Russ and I were married by my brother, a minister, on the lawn of my family's summer cabin at Peach Lake, Brewster, New York. We've renewed our vows there on the rare occasion when we were back on our anniversary date. My family owned that cabin for 40 years and pieces of my life are there. I can still hear the creaking of the dock every time I took that last step before diving in.

Every Labour Day, we gathered for my uncle's birthday, with a big ham, Mom's macaroni and cheese, farm-fresh corn on the cob and tomatoes, chocolate cake and Toll House cookies. We squeezed around the long table on the screened porch, and later, as the grandchildren started coming, spilled out onto the new deck as well.

When I go back to the lake now, after years of living in BC's coniferous zone, I notice with sweet nostalgia how the late-afternoon light shimmers through the leaves of the deciduous trees. It's a translucent light that filters through the delicate, skin-taut veins and broad leaves of the maples and elms; it casts a Renoir-type of unfocused haze. It is the light of my childhood, youth and coming-of-age years. When Bruce told me his cabin story, a part of me smiled in recognition and a part of me ached for the past.

2 1

A Hut of My Own

->->->-<-<-

*This wasn't a bad idea, I thought, to have the family in one house,
while I would live some distance away in a hut with a pile of books
and a writing table, and an open fire where I would roast
chestnuts and cook my soup on a tripod.*

CARL JUNG, Swiss psychologist

->-<-

WHEN WE MOVED to our present home on the fringes of Victoria, I was quite enraptured by the "mountain" behind our house: a treed hillside with a tangle of vegetation and forest, leading to an open plateau area. It was here, on this plateau, that I wanted my hut. For my whole writer's life, I've envied those with a refuge, a hut, a place to go and create. And finally, I had a perfect location for such a venture.

Composer Gustav Mahler had a hut, I've been told, near his summer home in Maiernigg, Germany, where he wrote his 7th Symphony, and even Queen Victoria is said to have slipped away when she could to a simple shepherd's hut that she and Prince Albert discovered in Scotland.

Now, my hut is actually there, waiting for me on the Plateau of the Muses, my name for the level area where it stands. Its existence is a humbling realization.

The being of my hut is the miracle that it finally exists as a physical presence,

about two and a half metres square. It was assembled by Russ and me, carefully finished and spartanly furnished. It is.

The essence of the hut is something completely different. It is a spiritual cleansing that affects me each time I approach the plateau where it perches, partway over a small cliff. The essence of "huttedness" includes tranquility, beauty, simplicity, mindfulness, connectedness, creativity, repose, solitude and awareness of other, as well as of self.

I find I've started to think in terms of our need, as a society, for huttedness, which may simply be another term for sacred place. My hut represents my own creative corner of the universe, and that's part of what I cherish, but there is something more: the transformation that occurs with each pilgrimage up to it. The three-minute walk through the woods is a thankfulness ritual, a meditation, a rejoicing. A wake-up call for what is needed for maintenance of my soul.

◄ The hut.

▶ Russ and his mandolin at the hut.

One evening, when I was upset, ranting, angry and hurt, Russ said, "Let's go up to the hut." There, amidst fog and clouds eerie and mystical, I found peace. It always seems windier up at the hut, but in truth I love the soughing of the trees, the tinkling of wind chimes and the womb-like atmosphere within as the wind swirls around outside. This is, in many ways, my sacred centre. I have a better appreciation now for Buddhist monks who trek up a path to a dharma centre. This is my monastery.

The walk through the cool green forest, up, up, brushing past patches of lush, thick moss that shimmers yellow-green in the sun, passing underneath Douglas fir and cedars, and beside muscular arbutus and bright fluorescent-red currant bushes, meandering up the winding path, slowly climbing, is a physical manifestation of my desire to seek the light. The hike is a transitional time when I work my way up to a different plateau of being.

July evening. The pink sky glow is nearly gone. A train whistle blows. I drink in the fir-fragrant air. A bell chimes. I watch the stages of the lovely arbutus— just now, the bark peeling in big pieces, the leaves, brittle and dry, fall and litter the path. July heat. 9:30 PM. The pink is all but finished. A slight breeze cools my face and blows away the mosquito at my ear. A dog barks. A mother's voice carries up the hill.

August. An exquisite hut moment—the long slanted rays fan across the plateau, spill onto the mostly dried mosses, cast a golden glow on the cedar of the hut—a spot bathed in light. "Jesus rays" (as photographers refer to them) of gold streaming into the darkness of a Rembrandt, where all is hazy, solemn, dim, save the dazzling beam.

Over time, my hut has become a touchstone, my place of refuge and refreshment. Years of use, along with repeated times of healing, have imbued it with a sacredness that increases with each time of solace, each hour of quietude, each intentional walk to the plateau.

When members of my family came west for Holly and Dean's wedding a few years ago, my sister Emmy collected twigs and curved branches and formed a heart on the knoll across from the hut. When I sit on the small deck of the hut— our favourite place for picnic suppers—and look across at the view of the hills beyond, the knoll is in my line of sight. The stick heart is still there.

In fact, I mend my broken heart, both literally and metaphorically, every time I go up to the hut. The first thing I do each time I arrive on the plateau is rearrange those sticks, which have usually been blown apart by the frequent winds, and rebuild my heart on the hill. Then I begin to mend my own heart, simply by allowing myself to sink gratefully into the grace, beauty and simplicity of that spot.

One of my favourite hut memories is my mother's visit in June 2003. We decided to take Mom, then 87, up to the plateau, despite her difficulty walking, since she was determined to see my hut. We drove up a nearby driveway and began the trek across the uneven, rocky plateau with her granddaughters Holly and Kristi on either side of Mom, supporting her under her arms. I walked behind with a lawn chair, in case she needed to sit down to rest or lost her balance, and Dad, 90, followed carefully behind me.

But we made it—and I'll never forget Mom's sense of accomplishment and joy as she and Dad sat in the hut doorway with Holly and Kristi and posed for photos of the event. We had a snack, and Mom marvelled at the beauty of the spot, and told us again how she likes to be able "to picture" the places we talk about, and now she could picture the hut. Each of us knew this was a significant moment, a future memory.

A couple of weeks after my parents' visit, in one of those slightly worrisome follow-up mammograms, the doctor found a lump in my breast and performed a biopsy. This was a bit ominous, but worst of all was waiting for five days to get the results. During that endless weekend, Russ and I retreated to my hut. I remember vividly—I can still feel it—the soothing effect that spot had on both of us. By this point, we were in a swirl of inner turmoil, steeling ourselves for biopsy results that my own GP had already warned me did not look good. We had hardly slept, were clinging to tiny shreds of hope, but in my heart I think we already knew the answer.

Despite all this, at one of the most frightening and chaotic moments of my life, as Russ and I spent time at the hut, I could feel a calmness begin to infuse each of us. I sat writing in my journal in a chair on the tiny front deck overlooking the hills, and Russ stretched out on his back on the grassy knoll across from me, looking up at the sky. We were quiet. We allowed ourselves to let go of the fears we felt and knew we had to face, and we momentarily stepped outside of the crisis we faced. I remember being amazed that I could feel this calm and peaceful in the midst of the storm that threatened to knock us flat.

It was a transformational moment that let me know that it would be possible to feel this way again, sometime in the future. I felt a sense of relief, and it taught me something about the strength we discover within ourselves when we need it, but also about the power of place to allow us to gain access to that deepest part of ourselves.

As I've gone through the process of writing this book, my understanding of how I respond to the *genius loci* in our part of the world has become clearer. I've seen how, in times of personal crisis, I need to go to the places that renew and calm me. We all need havens that feel safe, where nothing is expected of us, and where, despite our solitude, we feel connected to others and to the natural world.

And then there's the cancer thing. There is no doubt that we take a wider, deeper look at people and places when we face a life-threatening disease or situation or, for that matter, in any of life's most critical moments, and I've seen the way that place can be an expression of self and beyond myself—a link to the divine, the otherworld.

Again, more recently, I turned to my sacred place when my heart was heavy with worry. I've discovered it's one thing to go through a serious illness yourself, but quite another to go through it when someone you love is ill. In my experience, and I think most people would agree, it's far worse when you are the helpless bystander.

There were times when I didn't think my heart could handle the pain. But I knew with certainty that what I needed was to go home and just be at my hut. Especially in springtime, the hut and its surroundings are magnificent. Sitting among the wildflowers on our hillside each spring, when the sun filters through in the evening and the fragile camas petals are backlit to a wondrous purple-pink-cerulean hue, often brings tears to my eyes.

So, when the moment was right, I slipped away from hospitals and doctors and went home. I walked through the trees, passed the miniature Buddhas along the way and as always, rubbed their bellies and sent healing thoughts to people in my life who were seriously ill. Unfortunately, there is no dearth of candidates, ever. But this time, it was easy to choose where my mantras and prayers should be sent. And I knew I could also use some of those healing mantras myself.

In a cool, forested area beside the path under some larger trees, there is a dark patch where each year I spy two, three, maybe even four delicate calypso orchids. These shy little flowers grow singly, almost hidden, in the deepest shade.

◄ (*Left*) Common Camus, (*right*) death camus. PHOTOS BY LESLEY PRESTON AND STAR WEISS.

▼ Easter lilies. PHOTO BY LESLEY PRESTON.

► (Overleaf) Shooting star. PHOTO BY LESLEY PRESTON.

There they were again, sure enough, so fragile I always fear they will be trampled.

Just beyond the orchids, past a scattering of shooting stars, I climbed up the short, steep pitch and onto the plateau. I gasped and exclaimed at the wondrous display, so temporal, so ephemeral, so glorious. I had done it, that is, managed to get there during that brief window of time when the sultry purple-blue camas were at their height.

Because of our annual culling of the notorious Scotch broom that threatens to take over any untamed ground in our region, our field of wildflowers has become wider and wilder every year. This year, the camas were more prolific than ever, undulating across the hilly meadow top, bordered by the brilliant yellow of spring gold and the deep fuchsia of sea blush. A carefully woven Persian carpet of pink and yellow and blue.

My heart was broken, so I tended to it first, carefully realigning the twigs and sticks that were out of place, and recreating a perfect heart. Then, as always, I opened the latch and went inside my little hut, inhaling the sweet cedar scent. Next, I took my traditional plateau walkabout, gingerly, for fear of treading on any of the tiny little flowers underfoot.

I found the skeleton of the deer that had died on the plateau a few months earlier, an event that brought bald eagles swooping close for about a week. I walked from one side of the plateau to the other and observed the way the sun's angle affects colour, and how the light changes almost minute by minute, especially in the long-shadowed rays of early evening.

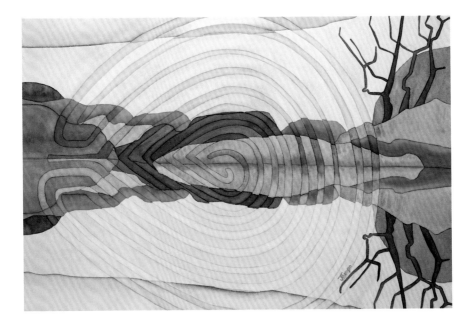

In telling stories for this book, many people have eloquently defined the attributes of a sacred place. There have been simple definitions like "a place of goodness" or "a safe place," and more ethereal definitions such as "an intersection between Heaven and Earth" or "a portal to the sacred, something much larger than ourselves." Sister Joyce Harris said, "The air is electric," containing both creative energy and stillness, a place to find calmness and peace. Her observation that "everything is sacred" but the sacredness is heightened in certain mysterious places could easily apply to the First Nations' feelings at traditional bathing sites, or the Wiccan belief in the "holiest of holy" space found within a cast circle.

When discussing what makes a place sacred, people often mentioned the importance of being part of a community, one that is "honest about our fragility" and "open to moments of tenderness," or one that is "happy, getting up and dancing." A sacred place can also be a community where people reveal their suffering in a safe haven—for many people a sacred place is a place for healing the heart.

The feeling of being in a space "that gives you permission to be all you are"— where you are accepted unconditionally—and are attuned to what is around you seems to be an essential part of sacredness. That's the way I feel about my hut.

When I heard Michael McCarthy or other First Nations people talk about the sacred knowledge that comes from their ancestors and their long relationship with the land, I confess I was a bit envious. I'm a wandering, non-Native person

◄ Camas labyrinth. JOANNE THOMSON

with little access to ancestral roots. Maybe part of my quest is to find a sense of rootedness. Someone asked me, "How is rooted different than sacred?" If one of the criteria for sacredness is a place of continuity and connectedness that links us to a greater consciousness, perhaps of the Creator, then going to places where people feel linked to the ancestors is a journey to their sacred roots. I've been deeply affected when people told me stories of the presence of the ancestors at sacred sites. I know this is their truth and believe they have a wisdom and way of knowing that I don't possess.

A non-Native woman told me about walking near Tsa-kwa-luten Lodge on Quadra Island a few years ago when, to her surprise, she saw a vision of Native people gathered around a fire on the beach. When she repeated this story to a First Nations friend, the person merely smiled and said, "You're very sensitive." I keep hearing stories like this. I've been trained to believe in empirical evidence only, so that's my bias. However, as I get older, it's becoming clearer to me that there are many things I don't know or am only beginning to understand. It's as though we've lost the connection, but in little spurts, we can feel the current briefly again.

Immersion in water represents a sacred cleansing for cultures around the world, and it's interesting to hear repeated mention of ritual bathing, in the Salmon River and other rivers, ponds or streams, or even the ocean, an act that is still important to many of our coastal First Nations. One friend took me to a sacred bathing site used by his people for hundreds of years. The location of sacred baths is often kept secret, so I felt honoured to be guided there. It was clear that being at that spot affected my companion, who talked about feeling a presence as we stood beside the tranquil water, the sunlight filtering through cedar branches overhead. Another friend told me that she always feels the healing spirit of her grandmother at the baths, and goes there purposefully to feel that connection. The sacred baths are still used regularly, quietly, secretly and deserve to be protected and preserved.

Many, many people told me they find the sacred in nature (trees, rivers, the sea, mountains, beaches), which reconfirms the research findings of those like

Gail Wells who have studied these trends. And which, by the way, is proof that the spiritual geography of the magnificent, wild province of British Columbia *does* affect us profoundly. Gail has found that many Cascadians find "awe and wonder" in the natural world; our experience of the divine can be based simply on our relationship with ancient trees. Could it be that anything that expands our awareness beyond our own lifespan is another link to the sacred?

I know there is a dichotomy in my searching. On the one hand, I'm passionate about this topic of sacred places, and I love the journey and the people I have met. On the other hand, I'm still the skeptic, or at least uncomfortable at times when I feel I'm hovering too close to the trendy New Age flame.

I've been changed by my journey in unexpected ways. You never know how the sacred will touch you personally, and that is perhaps a good lesson to learn. Occasionally, I have been able to see how things were moving forward in tandem and were interconnected. It was exciting to realize that the topic of sacred places was my "way in" to learn more about people's spirituality and values and beliefs. Just as years ago, on the TV show *Kitchen Culture*, the interest in ethnic foods was the "way in" for me and for the viewers to learn more about cultural diversity and human commonality.

Sometimes, indications of societal trends emerged from individual stories. The labyrinth motif is becoming more widely known and used, partly because of our growing interest in exploring meditative and physical experiences as a way to feel closer to the divine. A labyrinth is a good way to bring in both contemplative and active practices. I've learned to appreciate the intentional act of walking a labyrinth as a widely accessible metaphor for existence.

I sometimes wonder why I keep running into delightful, perceptive Catholic nuns, who seem to somehow be playing significant cameo roles in my personal drama. Maybe Sister Sheila Moss's observation that it is Catholic sisters who are leading the way in creation spirituality, which reinforces a belief in the divine in nature, honours the feminine, celebrates hope, and promotes social and ecological justice and interfaith understanding, that draws me to the sisters' lives and work.

At William Head Institution, the popularity of the talking circle parallels the rediscovery elsewhere in our society of the symbolism and strength of the circle: the proposed InterSpiritual Centre in Vancouver also plans to incorporate the circle design in its main worship space.

-+->-<-+-

I FOUND IT fascinating to hear so many people, both inside and outside of organized faiths, refer to the history of a place, the repetition of rituals in a spot that leaves an energy people can feel in the present. Can a place capture the memory of human activity and hold it there? The notion is given credence in many sacred places around the world. Just talk to someone who has visited Iona, Scotland, or Chartres Cathedral in France or Yuquot, BC.

Martin Palmer, Secretary General of the Alliance of Religions and Conservation (ARC) in England, who conceived of the Sacred Land Project that has now spread around the world (see Appendix A) says we can identify sacred places by the splendour of the place, the history of the place or by that sense of the divine that we feel there. This sounds familiar: it seems that the concept of sacred land has started to penetrate the collective consciousness.

"We've always had the sense that the historical sites are the pinnacles, but everything is sacred. It's about resacralizing the everyday, making it a sacrament to be in nature," Martin said.

At a time when fundamentalism and religious zealotry seem to be flourishing, it is worth noting that many of us here in BC are on a different path: engaged in spiritual searches that are expansive and open, rather than narrowly defined, and that reflect our profound appreciation of our diverse landscape and our diverse population. We are finding ways to cherish and explore wildness. At the same time, we are recognizing the importance of establishing a home base, a place where we feel part of a community we care about. As Murray Groom put it, we are discovering our human need for both the tent and the temple.

When the chaplains and others attending a meeting at the UVic Interfaith

▶ The dancers, favourite arbutus trees near the hut. PHOTO BY LESLEY PRESTON

Chapel all agreed that the palpable sense of sacredness they experience in the building was due in part to the spiritual energies of the many different faith groups that met there, it made me feel excited, hopeful. Somehow, through a glass darkly, I'm more and more aware of a movement forward—tectonic plates shifting ever so slightly toward a more cohesive universe. A bit silly, I guess. Naive, perhaps. But persistent. Not to be denied.

Several people I talked to, including Louise Mangan, minister of the post-denominational Pacific InterChristian Community—a community that shares devotion to spiritual practices, rather than to one organized religious identity—believe that in the postmodern age we live in (the time of electronic media, ecological awareness and openness to mysticism, ancient wisdom and spiritual-ity), we are moving beyond the divisiveness of separate dogmas and looking for a more universal and inclusive way to honour the sacred in our midst. Finding the divine in nature is often a big part of that. As Mark Shibley would say, people are "differently"—not less—religious today than in the past.

Over and over, I heard people say that it is possible to discover a sense of the sacred almost anywhere, if we come with intention and awe. Many feel that the intentionality they bring to a space—a feeling of grace or reverence "where change can happen"—affects the aura of the spot and can transform it to hallowed ground. Maybe we are beginning to walk side by side as we follow our various religious and ethical paths (as Joseph Campbell put it, "Different software, same hardware," or words to that effect) and are beginning to slowly realize that we all need to walk softly and carefully on this wonderful but wounded planet.

Something's happenin' here … what it is ain't exactly clear.

"For What It's Worth," BUFFALO SPRINGFIELD

I have many places I consider sacred, and have added several more to the list, as I've been introduced to other people's sacred sites. The places included in this book are a part of my journey and perhaps will become part of yours as well. This collection is a serendipitous sampling of sacred places on the West Coast.

It has never aspired to be a comprehensive or equitable listing, and I know it is also an unfinished symphony.

As I've learned about the traditional and non-traditional ways we are fulfilling our spiritual needs—whether by walking through the forest, sitting in a talking circle, or touring the Jamatkhana—I've been doing what I love: spending time with interesting, thoughtful people who shared with me their sacred places, the places that help them feel closer to that-which-matters-most.

Numerous people are eloquently defending the macrocosm—the necessity to save the whole Earth. That's what the worldwide environmental movement is all about, and the discussion of sacred places is a part of that conversation. I've concentrated here on the microcosm, the zoom-in close-up, where one anecdote represents the greater picture. Maybe together we can figure out the puzzle and jigsaw our way to an assembled whole.

My pilgrimage has taken me from prison to pinnacle, from lake to labyrinth, from synagogue to Skedans. Instead of the motley crew that Chaucer assembled at the Tabard Inn to tell the Canterbury Tales, I asked a variety of modern-day British Columbians to relate their "Cascadia Tales" of sacred places on the Pacific Coast. Their narratives reflect the eclectic spiritual mix of the pioneers, pilgrims and indigenous peoples who make up our population. The resulting tapestry is rich, a colourful weaving unfolding in the Canadian province that exists between East and West, dramatically perched on the Pacific Rim.

My journeys along the coast have taken me to new places, geographically and intellectually, and the implications of what I've learned are more far-reaching than I had expected. I believe that recognizing our personal sacred places affects how we see and relate to the world. Saving the whole globally warmed planet can be a daunting proposition. For some of us, one viable way to approach the universal challenge of tending to Gaia, the living, sacred Earth that needs our protection, is in bite-sized pieces. Why not start with the particular, the individual, the personal piece that touches our lives? Start with our chosen sanctuaries, the sacred places we care about deeply. Move on from there.

APPENDIX A
The Sacred Land Project

THE IDEA THAT it is time to identify, cherish and preserve sacred places is gaining popularity around the world. In the United Kingdom, the number of recognized sacred sites has been growing significantly in recent years, partly as a result of the Sacred Land Project (SLP).

The SLP, launched in 1997, is run by the Alliance of Religions and Conservation (ARC), a secular body that helps religious groups develop environmental programs. In 2001, the project went international, and now, 35 countries, including Mexico, Norway, France, Nepal, Ethiopia and China, have started similar or related projects. The SLP is one method of conserving and creating special places, and perhaps there are possibilities for similar ventures here in Canada.

Religious historian and theologian Martin Palmer is Secretary General of the ARC and the man who thought of the Sacred Land Project (SLP). In his book *The Spiritual Traveler* (originally the official guidebook of the SLP), he says the Sacred Land Project "seeks to enable local communities to recover, restore, or create sacred sites in their own locale. Such sites may be places of great antiquity such as pilgrimage routes or holy wells. Or they may be the creation of sacred space—a garden or a place of quiet reflection—in urban inner city areas."[1]

For example, the Jamyang Buddhist Centre, formerly an abandoned courthouse in a poor section of South London, has become, with assistance from the ARC, a vibrant meditation centre and meeting place, with a sacred garden just outside its doors.

The ARC website states, "Anywhere can be a sacred site—it only requires us to see our land as special and we will learn to tread more gently upon it."[2]

Martin, recently appointed special advisor to the United Nations Secretary General's team on Climate Change, the Environment, and the Faiths, says he is "fascinated by the relationship between history and belief; landscape and ecology. My spirituality—a great deal expressed through Christianity, with a dash of Taoism and Buddhism—is actually grounded in my homeland. My spiritual quest is driven by the land."

Several years ago, Martin was entertaining guests from India and China, and took his visitors sightseeing to Pennant Melangell, a traditional Celtic church in Wales built on a Bronze Age burial mound. His visitors were deeply moved, pointing out that there were places right there in Britain that were "as spiritual as any in the world."

"I just didn't see it," Martin said. But it is sometimes hard to appreciate what is right in front of us. (Maybe this is a lesson for us here in British Columbia.) When the Sacred Land Project got under way shortly afterwards, public reaction throughout Britain was "astonishing."

"We got the notion into the blood system," and soon the idea that "nobody lives more than ten miles away from a sacred site" was resulting in hundreds of local sacred land initiatives across the United Kingdom.

"We hit at the right moment, and we hit something very deep in the British." One important element was that the project supported the creation of *new* sites, not just historic, traditional churchyards or stone circles.

APPENDIX B

Further Explorations

CHAPTER ONE • *Haida Gwaii: A Place of Spirit*

You can fly or take a ferry to Haida Gwaii, and from Queen Charlotte City go by
floatplane or boat to Skedans or Ninstints.
Queen Charlotte Visitor Information: 250-559-8316 or info@qcinfo.ca;
http://www.qcinfo.ca.

Balance Rock is on the beach just north of Skidegate and is visible from the road.

Websites to visit:
http://www.robertbateman.ca
http://www.farahnosh.com.

CHAPTER TWO • *What Is Sacred?*

Directions to Myra Falls: Head north on the Island Highway (Route 1)
to Campbell River. Go west on Highway 28 to the entrance to Strathcona Provincial
Park. Proceed down Buttle Lake Road (bear and deer live here) past Buttle Narrows
Bridge and toward Strathcona-Westmin Park. You'll see signs for Myra Falls. The hike
in is about 10–15 minutes. There are good rocky outcrops for picnics or photos,
midway down the falls.

CHAPTER THREE • *Bumping Into St. Clare's Monastery*

The sisters welcome parishioners and visitors to morning mass and morning prayer.
Street and mailing address:
St. Clare's Monastery, 2359 Calais Road, Duncan, BC, V9L 5V5;
250-748-2232 or poorclare@highspeedplus.com;
http://www.poorclares.ca.

CHAPTER FOUR • *Walking the Labyrinth*

Meg Hansen, labyrinth facilitator: 250-749-6770 or yourtime@telus.net.

Joanne Thomson, labyrinth workshops on the beach (and other courses):
250-881-1539 or joannedthomson@shaw.ca;
http://members.shaw.ca/joannedthomson.

Christ Church Cathedral Labyrinth is located beside the cathedral at:
930 Burdett Avenue, Victoria, BC, v8v 3G8; 250-383-2714;
http://www.christchurchcathedral.bc.ca.

To book the University of Victoria's portable labyrinth: 250-721-8338
or chaplain@uvic.ca; or contact Henri Lock: 250-472-4159 or hlock@uvic.ca;
http://wweb.uvic.ca/interfaith

Victoria Community Labyrinth Society: 250-380-2838 (Aryana)
or victoriaLabyrinth@shaw.ca.

CHAPTER FIVE • *Cascadia Tales: The Wanderer's Path to the Sacred*

Directions to the mouth of Shawnigan Creek:
Head north on the Island Highway (Route 1), turn right at Mill Bay onto
Deloume Road as far as the stop sign. Turn left onto Lashburn Road,
drive to the end, park, and look for the footpath to the stairs.

Sylvan United Church is located at:
985 Shawnigan-Mill Bay Road, Mill Bay, BC, v0r 2P2;
250-743-4659 or Admin@SylvanUnited.ca;
http://www.sylvanunited.ca.

CHAPTER SIX • *The Songs Stay There Forever: First Nations Sacred Sites*

Directions to Garry Point Park:
Head west from Highway 99 via Steveston Highway, turn left (south) on 7th Avenue
to Garry Point Park.

CHAPTER SEVEN • *A Different Kind of Sacred*

Unitarian Church of Vancouver is located at:
949 West 49th Avenue (at Oak), Vancouver, BC, v5z 2t1; 604-261-7204;
http://vancouver.unitarians.ca/cms/site/pid/1.

CHAPTER EIGHT • *Mountains*

Mount Albert Edward is located on Forbidden Plateau in Strathcona Provincial Park.
Directions from Courtenay:
Follow signs north to Mount Washington ski area, proceed to ski area and
follow signs to Nordic Lodge. Park before you reach the lodge, at the signs to Forbidden
Plateau and Paradise Meadows. It's best to hike in to Kwai Lake or Circlet Lake and make
that your base camp for a hike up to the peak the next day.

John Dean Provincial Park is located on the slopes of LA'U WELNEW,
2 km west of East Saanich Road, near Sidney. The park can be accessed off of
Highway 17. Turn west onto McTavish Road, then south onto East Saanich Road,
then follow John Dean Road west to the park. John Elliott's advice to park visitors to
the park is to be aware that you may come upon a ceremony, and if you do, be careful
and respectful, leave people alone, and don't interrupt or talk to them.

YAAS Mountain is located above and to the west of the Malahat Highway, south of
Mill Bay.

CHAPTER NINE • *Prayerful Places: Large, Small and Personal*

Burnaby Ismaili Jamatkhana and Centre is located at:
4010 Canada Way, Burnaby, BC, v5g 1g8.
Group tours of 10 or more people may be arranged;
604-438-4010 (Office hours). Naz Rayani organizes bus tours from Victoria to the
Burnaby Jamatkhana periodically; ynr@shaw.ca;
Further info: http://www.csrs.uvic.ca.

Directions to Quadra Island United Church:
From Campbell River, BC, take the ferry to Quadra, drive up the hill take the first right onto Green Road and follow it to Cape Mudge village. Drive through the village until you see the church. Services are held Sundays at 11 AM. If you wish to gain access to the church: 250-285-3473 (ask for Alberta).

The modern cedar building with totems past the Quadra Island United Church is the Nuyumbalees Cultural Centre (formerly the Kwaguilth Museum); 250-285-3733; museum hours vary in winter; starting in May 2008, the museum will be open seven days a week.

CHAPTER TEN • *The Sacred Forest*

Cathedral Grove is located 30 km west of Parksville, on Highway 4 (toward Port Alberni).

Reginald Hill Trail, Salt Spring Island:
Trailhead at Reginald Hill strata development (1 km south of Fulford ferry terminal at end of Morningside Road). Park outside gate, then walk through gate, take first driveway on the left, and follow red metal markers to the trailhead .

Directions to Carmanah Walbran:
From Lake Cowichan, follow South Shore Road past Gordon Bay Provincial Park to the Nitinat Main Road, or follow the North Shore Road through Youbou to the Nitinat Main Road. Continue along Nitinat Main Road till it connects with Junction South. Turn left onto South Main and proceed to the Caycuse River Bridge. Cross the bridge, turn right onto Rosander Main for approximately 29 km to the park

Directions to Burgoyne Bay Provincial Park, Salt Spring Island:
From Fulford Harbour head north to Burgoyne Bay Road, turn left, head west to the bay.

Directions to Witty's Lagoon Regional Park, Metchosin, Victoria:
From the Old Island Highway (Route 1A), head west on Sooke Road to Metchosin Road, turn left. Park entrance is approximately 6 km on left.

Directions to Francis/King Regional Park, located 13 km west of downtown Victoria (a 30-minute drive) via the Trans-Canada Highway (Route 1):
Turn right on Helmcken Road and left on West Burnside, then right on Prospect Lake Road to Munn Road where the park appears on the right.

Pacific Spirit Regional Park is located in Vancouver on Point Grey, east of the University of British Columbia. Numerous accesses exist to park trails via the UBC campus and Southwest Marine Drive and 16th Avenue.

CHAPTER ELEVEN • *Yuquot, Where the Wind Blows from All Directions*

To inquire about renting a cabin, camping on Nootka Island or information about Summerfest, call the Mowachaht/Muchalaht band office;
250-283-2015 or 1-800-238-2933, or reception@yuquot.ca;
http://www.yuquot.ca/index-2.html.

To book passage to Yuquot on the *Uchuck III*, call Nootka Sound Service;
250-283-2325 or info@mvuchuck.com;
http://www.mvuchuck.com.

CHAPTER TWELVE • *Bernice's Synagogue*

Congregation Emanu-El is located at:
1461 Blanshard Street, Victoria, BC, v8w 2J3.
The public is welcome at Saturday services (9 AM–12 noon).
Tours of the building are available year-round; 250-382-0615;
http://www.congregation-emanu-el.org/index.php.

CHAPTER THIRTEEN • *Shared Sacred Spaces*

The University of Victoria Interfaith Chapel and Finnerty Gardens is located adjacent to Parking Lot 6 at UVic. Open every weekday from 8:30 AM to 5:30 PM and can also be booked for weddings, funerals or special gatherings; 250-721-8022.

Interfaith Chaplaincy Services; 250-721-8338 or chaplain@uvic.ca;
http://web.uvic.ca/interfaith.

Whistler Village Church is located at Maurice Young Millennium Place:
4335 Blackcomb Way, Whistler, BC, V0N 1B4.
Sunday services at: 10 AM; 604-935-8450 or wvchurch@shawcable.com;
http://www.whistlervillagechurch.com.

InterSpiritual Centre: 604-720-5045 (board chair Louise Mangan)
or lmangan@telus.net;
http://www.interspiritual.org/contact.html.

CHAPTER FOURTEEN • *Providence Farm: A Place of Compassion*

Directions to Providence Farm:
From Duncan, head east on Trunk Road to 1843 Tzouhalem Road,
Duncan, BC, V9L 5L6, just before St. Ann's Church.
Tours, facility rentals, and wedding bookings available;
250-746-4204 or provfarm@providence.bc.ca;
http://www.providence.bc.ca.

CHAPTER FIFTEEN • *Retreat*

Queenswood Centre is located at 2494 Arbutus Road, Victoria, BC, V8N 1V8;
250-477-3822 (for more info or to register for programs) or
info@queenswoodcentre.com;
http://www.queenswoodcentre.com

Glenairley Centre for Earth and Spirit:
6040 East Sooke Road, Sooke, BC, V9Z 0Z7;
250-642-3546 (for more info) or gces@telus.net;
http://www.centreforearthandspirit.org.

Hollyhock is located on Cortes Island: From the ferry head south on Sutil Point Road to Highfield Road; follow signs to Hollyhock; 800-933-6339 x232 or 250-935-6576 (for reservations) or registration@hollyhock.ca; http://www.hollyhock.ca/cms.

CHAPTER SIXTEEN • *Sacred Waters*

Fishermen's Memorial is located in Garry Point Park in Steveston, Richmond. (See directions under Chapter Six in this appendix.)

Locarno Beach is located in Vancouver, immediately east of the University of BC, along Northwest Marine Drive.

Rick Hansen Foundation: 1-800-213-2131 or info@rickhansen.com; http://www.rickhansen.com.

Directions to Ogden Point, Victoria: Head south on Douglas Street (Highway 1) to Dallas Road, turn right, go 1.5 km west to the Ogden Point Breakwater.

University of Victoria Interfaith Chapel: See directions in Chapter Thirteen.

Directions to Long Beach: From Port Alberni, take Highway 4 west to Tofino/Ucluelet and Pacific Rim National Park. From Port Alberni it takes about one and a half hours to Ucluelet and the beginning of Long Beach, and about two hours to Tofino. From Victoria the trip to the Long Beach and Tofino area is about four and a half hours.

Directions to Sombrio Beach: From Sooke, head west on Renfrew Road. After crossing Loss Creek Bridge, watch for signs to Sombrio Beach access (easy to miss! Watch carefully!) and turn left down a rough gravel road. Ten-minute walk to the beach from parking lot.

CHAPTER SEVENTEEN • *Gardens Private and Public*

The display of cherry blossoms in Victoria is found throughout the city, from March to May; favourite areas include Moss Street and South Turner Street. In April, recommended areas include James Bay (Irving Park, or Niagara Street between Dock and Oswego streets), Beacon Hill Park, and the Japanese Garden in Hatley Park at Royal Roads University.

CHAPTER EIGHTEEN • *The Unexpected*

William Head Institution, Metchosin; 250-391-7000 (general inquiries).

Jericho Beach Park (venue of the Vancouver Folk Music Festival) is located immediately west of Hastings Mill Park at the westerly end of Point Grey Road. Other access points via West 4th Avenue.
Vancouver Folk Music Festival; 604-602-9798;
http://www.thefestival.bc.ca.

Vancouver's Downtown Eastside is located southeast of Vancouver's Gastown District, between the docks and the train/bus terminal.

St. Paul's Parish Church is located at 381 E. Cordova Street, Vancouver, BC.
Mailing address and office location:
525 Campbell Ave, Vancouver, BC, V6A 3K5.
Sunday services at 11 AM, Tuesday–Friday at 11:30 AM; 604-254-3100;
http://www.rcav.bc.ca/parishes/times/st_pauls_van/index.htm.

CHAPTER NINETEEN • *Remembrance: Standing on the Threshold*

Directions to Sylvia Stark's gravesite, Salt Spring:
From the Fulford ferry terminal, drive into Ganges and through town until you come to Central Hall (where the cinema is located) on Lower Ganges Road. Park there, walk to the right, behind the hall, about 50 m or so. Sylvia Stark's grave is well marked.

Victoria Hospice is located on the 3rd floor of the Richmond Pavilion at the Royal Jubilee Hospital, 1952 Bay Street, Victoria, BC, v8r 1J8; 250-370-8715; http://www.victoriahospice.org/index.html.

See directions to Myra Falls under Chapter Two in this appendix.

CHAPTER TWENTY • *Home*

Website to visit for more information on Maarnada, the Schaddelees' home and studio: http://www.maarnada.ca.

CHAPTER TWENTY-ONE • *A Hut of My Own*

My hut is located on a sunny hillside just above my Metchosin home. My email is starweiss@shaw.ca and I'd love to hear from you.

CHAPTER TWENTY-TWO • *Sacred Stories*

Alliance for Religions and Society (ARC): http://www.arcworld.org/contact.htm.

Sacred Land Project: http://www.arcworld.org/projects.asp?projectID=9.

ENDNOTES

INTRODUCTION • *The Sacred Where of the British Columbia Coast*

1 Norris, Kathleen. Quoted from her online conversation about *Dakota: A Spiritual Geography*: http://www.houghtonmifflinbooks.com/readers_guides/norris_dakota.shtml.

CHAPTER ONE • *Haida Gwaii: A Place of Spirit*

1 Carr, Emily. *Klee Wyck*. Douglas & McIntyre, Vancouver, 1990. p. 51.

CHAPTER TWO • *What Is Sacred?*

1 Eliade, Mircea. *The Sacred and the Profane*. pp. 9–10.
2 Peterson, Natasha. *Sacred Sites*. n.p.

CHAPTER FIVE • *Cascadia Tales: The Wanderer's Path to the Sacred*

1 Marks, Lynne. Citing Census of Canada, 1901–2001, from her work *Leaving God Behind When They Crossed the Rocky Mountains: Exploring Unbelief in Turn-of-the-Century British Columbia*, now a chapter in the new book *Household Counts: Canadian Households and Families in 1901*. Edited by Eric W. Sager and Peter Baskerville. University of Toronto Press, 2006.
2 Todd, Douglas. *Cascadia: Spirituality, Geography and Social Change*. Paper presented August 24, 2006.
3 Statistics Canada Summer 2006 report, *Canadian Social Trends*. p. 3.
4 Marks, Lynne. Census of Canada, 1901–2001.
5 Block, Tina. *Everyday Infidels: A Social History of Secularism in the Postwar Pacific Northwest*. pp. 266–267.
6 Ibid.
7 Block, Tina. August 21, 2007, email.
8 Block, Tina. *Everyday Infidels*. p. iv.
9 Todd, Douglas. Speech "Shared Sacred Spaces," Wosk Centre for Dialogue, Simon Fraser University, February 9, 2006.

10   Wells, Gail. In phone conversations and emails (2007) and notes from Cascadia symposium (2006).

11   Killen, Patricia O'Connell. In phone conversations and emails (2007) and notes from Cascadia symposium (2006).

12   Shibley, Mark. "Sacred Nature: Earth-Based Spirituality as Popular Religion in the Secular Northwest" (unpublished article), and in phone conversations and emails (2007) and notes from Cascadia symposium (2006).

CHAPTER SIX • *The Songs Stay There Forever: First Nations Sacred Sites*

1   Spelling and definitions of SENCOTEN words as provided by Tom Sampson.

2   Spelling and definitions of Musqueam words as provided by Terry Point.

CHAPTER SEVEN • *A Different Kind of Sacred*

iv   Gerson, Wolfgang. "The Design of the Building and Grounds." p. 1.

2   Ibid.

3   Gerson, Wolfgang. "Looking through my church files of 1961 to 1964." n.p.

4   Gerson, Wolfgang. "The Design of the Building and Grounds." n.p.

5   Ibid.

6   Gerson, Wolfgang. "1989 Nov." n.p.

7   Gerson, Wolfgang. "Looking through my church files of 1961 to 1964." n.p.

8   Gerson, "1989 Nov." p. 1.

9   Gerson, "The Design of the Building and Grounds." p. 1.

10   Gerson, Wolfgang. "1989 Nov." n.p.

11   Hewett, A. Philip. *The Spirit to Be Expressed in a Unitarian Church Building.* p. 1.

12   "Info packet for design of church." pp. 5–6.

13   Gerson, Wolfgang. "Looking through my church files." n.p.

14   Gerson, Wolfgang. "Letter to Mr. Ian Gray." p. 2.

15   Gerson, Wolfgang. "Looking through my church files." n.p.

16   Gerson, Wolfgang. "Letter to Mr. Ian Gray." p. 3.

CHAPTER EIGHT • *Mountains*

1 Report of the First Nations Cultural Heritage Impact Assessment and Consultation, 1997, Section 2.1. pp. 1–2.
2 Ibid., Section 4.1. p. 1.

CHAPTER NINE • *Prayerful Places: Large, Small and Personal*

1 Assu, Harry. *Assu of Cape Mudge.* p. 93.

CHAPTER ELEVEN • *Yuquot, Where the Wind Blows from All Directions*

1 Mowachaht/Muchalaht First Nation. *Yuquot Agenda Paper* [*for the*] *Historic Sites and Monuments Board of Canada.* p. 9.
2 Ibid.
3 As paraphrased by Richard Inglis, September 2007.

CHAPTER TWELVE • *Bernice's Synagogue*

1 *The History of Congregation Emanu-El, Victoria, British Columbia* (pamphlet).

CHAPTER FOURTEEN • *Providence Farm: A Place of Compassion*

1 Spelling and translation provided by Ron George.

CHAPTER TWENTY-TWO • *Sacred Stories*

1 Eliade, Mircea. *The Sacred and the Profane.* p. 36.

APPENDIX A • *The Sacred Land Project*

1 Palmer, Martin. *The Spiritual Traveler.* p. xii.
2 Alliance of Religions and Conservation website:
   http://www.arcworld.org/projects.asp?projectID-55.

BIBLIOGRAPHY

BOOKS

Artress, Lauren. *The Sacred Path Companion: A Guide to Walking the Labyrinth to Heal and Transform*. Riverhead Books, 2006.

———. *Walking a Sacred Path: Rediscovering the Labyrinth as a Spiritual Tool*. Riverhead Books, 1995.

Assu, Harry, with Joy Inglis. *Assu of Cape Mudge: Recollections of a Coastal Indian Chief*. University of British Columbia Press, 1989.

Basho, Matsuo. *Basho's Journey: Literary Prose of Matsuo Basho*. State University of New York Press, 2005.

Bibby, Reginald W. *The Boomer Factor, What Canada's Most Famous Generation Is Leaving Behind*. Bastian Books, 2006.

Bloomsbury Dictionary of Quotations. Bloomsbury Publishing Limited, 1990.

Bolen, Jean Shinoda. *Crossing to Avalon*. HarperSanFrancisco, 1994.

Brussat, Frederic and Mary Ann. *Spiritual Literacy: Reading the Sacred in Everyday Life*. Touchstone, Simon & Schuster, 1996.

Carey, Neil G. *A Guide to the Queen Charlotte Islands*. Raincoast Books, 1998.

Carmichael, David, and Jane Hubert, Editors. *Sacred Sites, Sacred Places*. Routledge, 1997.

Carr, Emily. *Klee Wyck*. Douglas & McIntyre, 2003.

Carter, Velma, and Levero Carter. *The Black Canadians: Their History and Contributions*. Reidmore Books, 1993.

Chaucer, Geoffrey. *The Canterbury Tales, an Illustrated Edition*. Translated by Nevill Coghill. Prentice-Hall, 1986.

Coull, Cheryl. *A Traveller's Guide to Aboriginal BC*. Whitecap Books, 1996.

Cousineau, Phil. *The Art of Pilgrimage, The Seeker's Guide to Making Travel Sacred*. Conari Press, 1998.

Derry, Ramsay. *The World of Robert Bateman*. Madison Press Books, 1985.

Douglass, Don, and Reanne Hemingway-Douglass. *Exploring Vancouver Island's West Coast*, 2nd Edition. Fine Edge Productions, 1999.

Downs, Barry. *Sacred Places, British Columbia's Early Churches*. Douglas & McIntyre, 1980.

Eliade, Mircea. *The Sacred and the Profane, the Nature of Religion*. Harper Torchbooks, 1959.

Fox, Matthew. *Confessions: The Making of a Post-Denominational Priest*. Harper Collins, 1996.

———. *A New Reformation: Creation Spirituality and the Transformation of Christianity*. Inner Traditions, 2006.

Gayton, Don. *Landscapes of the Interior, Explorations of Nature and the Human Spirit*. New Society Publishers, 1996.

Geoffrion, Jill Kimberly Hartwell. *Living the Labyrinth: 101 Paths to a Deeper Connection with the Sacred*, Pilgrim Press. Geoffrion, 2000.

Gibson, Katherine. *Pause, Putting the Brakes on a Runaway Life*. Insomniac Press, 2006.

———. *Unclutter Your Life: Transforming Your Physical, Mental and Emotional Space*. Atria Books/Beyond Words, 2004.

Gill, Ian. *Haida Gwaii: Journeys Through the Queen Charlotte Islands*. Raincoast Books, 2004.

Harbord, Heather. *Nootka Sound and the Surrounding Waters of Maquinna*. Heritage House, 1996.

Horwood, Dennis, and Tom Parkin. *Haida Gwaii: The Queen Charlotte Islands*. Heritage House, 2000.

Hull, Fritz, Editor. *Earth and Spirit, the Spiritual Dimension of the Environmental Crisis*. Continuum Books, 1993.

Jonaitis, Aldona. *The Yuquot Whalers' Shrine*. University of Washington Press and Douglas & McIntyre in Canada, 1999.

Jones, Laurie. *Nootka Sound Explored: A West Coast History*. Ptarmigan Press, 1991.

Joseph, Frank, Editor. *Sacred Sites of the West, a Guide to Mystical Centers*. Hancock House, 1997.

Kramer, Pat. *Native Sites in Western Canada*. Altitude Publishing Canada, 1994.

Ladinsky, Daniel, Translator. *Love Poems from God, Twelve Sacred Voices from the East and West*. Penguin Books, 2002.

Lane, Patrick. *There Is a Season, a Memoir*. McClelland & Stewart, 2004.

Macdonald, Mary, Editor. *Experiences of Place*. Center for the Study of World Religions. Harvard Divinity School, 2003.

McLuhan, T. C. *Cathedrals of the Spirit, the Message of Sacred Places*. HarperCollins, 1996.

Matthews, W. H. *Mazes and Labyrinths; a General Account of Their History and Development*. (No publisher listed), 1922.

Miller, Sherrill. *The Pilgrim's Guide to the Sacred Earth, a Companion Book*. Western Producer Prairie Books, 1991.

Milne, Courtney. *The Sacred Earth*. Viking, 1992.

———. *Sacred Places in North America, a Journey into the Medicine Wheel*. Stewart, Tabori & Chang, 1995.

Norris, Kathleen. *The Cloister Walk*. Riverhead Books, 1996.

———. *Dakota, a Spiritual Geography*. Houghton Mifflin, 1993.

O'Connell, Nicholas. *On Sacred Ground, the Spirit of Place in Pacific Northwest Literature*. University of Washington Press, 2003.

———. *At the Field's End: Interviews with 22 Pacific Northwest Writers*. University of Washington Press, 1998.

Palmer, Martin, and David Manning. *Sacred Gardens: A Guide to the Traditions, Meaning, and Design of Beautiful and Tranquil Places*. Piatkus, 2000.

Palmer, Martin, and Nigel Palmer. *The Spiritual Traveler—England, Scotland, Wales, the Guide to Sacred Sites and Pilgrim Routes in Britain* (formerly published as *Sacred Britain, a Guide to the Sacred Sites and Pilgrimage Routes of England, Scotland, and Wales*). HiddenSpring, 2000.

Palmer, Martin, with Victoria Finlay. *Faith in Conservation, New Approaches to Religions and the Environment*. The World Bank, Washington, DC, 2003.

Peterson, Natasha. *Sacred Sites: A Traveler's Guide to North America's Most Powerful Mystical Landmarks*. Contemporary Books, 1988.

Pojar, Jim and Andy MacKinnon. *Plants of the Pacific Northwest Coast*. Lone Pine, 1994.

Reekie, Jocelyn, and Annette Yourk. *Shorelines, Memoirs and Tales of the Discovery Islands*. Kingfisher Publishing, 1995.

Roberts, Elizabeth, and Eilas Amidon. *Life Prayers from Around the World*. HarperSan Francisco, 1996.

Sager, Eric W., and Peter Baskerville, Editors. *Household Counts: Canadian Households and Families in 1901*. Chapter: "Leaving God Behind When They Crossed the Rocky Mountains: Exploring Unbelief in Turn-of-the-Century British Columbia," by Lynne Marks. University of Toronto Press, 2006.

Saward, Jeff. *Magical Paths, Labyrinths and Mazes in the 21st Century*. Mitchell Beazley, 2002.

Sear, John F. *Sacred Places, American Tourist Attractions in the Nineteenth Century*. Oxford University Press, 1989.

Scott, Victoria, and Ernest Jones. *Sylvia Stark, a Pioneer*. Open Hand Publishing, 1991.

Shurcliff, Alice W., and Sarah Shurcliff Ingelfinger, Editors. *Captive of the Nootka Indians— the Northwest Coast Adventure of John R. Jewitt, 1802–1806*. Back Bay Books, 1993.

Smyly, John and Carolyn. *Those Born at Koona, the Totem Poles of the Haida Village Skedans, Queen Charlotte Islands*. Hancock House, 1994.

Swan, James A. *The Power of Place, Sacred Ground in Natural and Human Environments (Anthology)*. Quest Books, The Theosophical Publishing House, 1991.

———. *Sacred Places: How the Living Earth Seeks Our Friendship*. Bear & Company Publishing, 1990.

Suzuki, David. *The Sacred Balance, Rediscovering Our Place in Nature*. Greystone Books, 1997.

Todd, Douglas. *Brave Souls: Writers and Artists Wrestle with God, Love, Death and the Things That Matter*. Stoddart, 1996.

———, Editor. *Cascadia: The Elusive Utopia*. Ronsdale Press, 2008.

Turner, Victor and Edith. *Image and Pilgrimage in Christian Culture, Anthropological Perspectives*. Columbia University Press, 1978.

Veillette, John, and Gary White. *Early Indian Village Churches: Wooden Frontier Architecture in British Columbia*. University of British Columbia Press, 1977.

White, Evelyn. *Alice Walker: a Life*. WW Norton, 2004.

NEWSPAPERS AND MAGAZINE ARTICLES

Belperio, Pina. "Heritage of faith." *Pique, Newsmagazine*, February 24, 2005.

Collins, Gloria. "Metamorphosis, Sculptor Maarten Schaddelee." *Boulevard*, Summer, 1992.

Collins, Janet. "Spiritual journeys, One of the hottest travel trends today is one of the oldest." *Vancouver Sun*, Travel Section, May 26, 2007.

Crenna, Carol. "Rick Hansen, a Man Who's Always in Motion." *Vista Magazine*, Issue #39, March/April, 2005.

Heritage BC Newsletter. Articles on sacred buildings and spiritual places published leading up to Heritage Week, 2005.

Hoffman, Kitty. "Congregation Emanu-El Synagogue celebrates." *Times Colonist*, April 13, 2003.

McCulloch, Sandra. "Providence Farm aims to grow." *Times Colonist*, April 29, 2007.

Plunkett, Shelagh. "Victoria's Unsung Black Pioneers." *Boulevard*, #60.

Tafler, Sid. "Secrets of the Chiefs." *Monday Magazine*, Vol. 17, No. 11, March 7–13, 1991.

Tate, Brian. "Mowachaht/Muchalaht celebrates Yuquot Summerfest." *Ha-Shilth-Sa Newspaper*, August 25, 2004.

Timmermans, Mark. "Holy Ground." *Providence Community News*. May, 2007.

Weiss, Star. "The Healing Fields." *Harrowsmith*, June, 1994.

———. "Poor Clares lead rich private lives." *Islander Magazine*, July 25, 1993.

———. "Harnessing the power of prayer." *Saturday Review*, August 7, 1993.

SPEECHES

Todd, Douglas. Speech on Shared Sacred Spaces, Wosk Centre for Dialogue, Simon Fraser University, February 9, 2006.

WEBSITES

Alice & Zora: An Interview with Valerie Boyd and Evelyn C. White:
http://www.inmotionmagazine.com/aco5/f_pride1.html.

Alliance for Religions and Conservation (ARC):
http://www.arcworld.org.

Carmanah Walbran Provincial Park:
http://www.env.gov.bc.ca/bcparks/explore/parkpgs/carmanah.html.

Carney, Pat. Encounters at Yuquot.
http://sen.parl.gc.ca/pcarney/english/SenatorPat/Coastal%20News/Yuquot.htm.

InterSpiritual Centre:
http://www.interspiritual.org/glance.html.

Labyrinth, St. Paul's Church, Vancouver:
http://www.stpaulsanglican.bc.ca/index.php?a=Labyrinth.

Louise and Sylvia Stark:
http://web.uvic.ca/history-robinson/cast/stark_ls.html.

Norris, Kathleen. Reader's Guide for *Dakota*:
http://www.houghtonmifflinbooks.com/readers_guides/norris_dakota.shtml.

Sacred Land Project:
http://www.arcworld.org/projects.asp?projectID=9.

Sylvia Estes Stark—Women in BC History, BC Archives Time Mac:
http://www.bcarchives.gov.bc.ca/exhibits/timemach/galler10/frames/stark.htm.

Sylvia Stark-Settler:
http://www.coolwomen.ca/coolwomen/cwsite.nsf/vwWeek.

Whistler Village Church:
   http://www.whistlervillagechurch.com/aboutus.html.

PAPERS, REPORTS, LETTERS, THESES, UNPUBLISHED PAPERS

Block, Tina. *Everyday Infidels: A Social History of Secularism in the Postwar Pacific North-west*. PhD dissertation, University of Victoria, Victoria, BC, 2006.

Fifty Year History of Congregation Emanu-El, A. As Seen Through the Eyes of Ralph Barer. Newsletter.

Gerson, Wolfgang. Unpublished letters: "Looking through my church files of 1961 to 1964"; "The Design of the Building and Grounds"; "1989, November"; "Letter to Mr. Ian Gray." (Courtesy Kate Gerson).

Groom, Murray. *The Role of the Guide in the Practice of Pilgrimage*. Doctor of Ministry dissertation, St. Stephen's College, Edmonton, Alberta, 2004.

Hewett, Philip. Unpublished report: *The Spirit to Be Expressed in a Unitarian Church Building*. (Courtesy Kate Gerson).

History of Congregation Emanu-El, Victoria, British Columbia, The. Pamphlet.

InterSpiritual Centre Architectural Survey Summary, March 8, 2006. Prepared by Acton Ostry Architects.

Providence Farm, a Therapeutic Community. AGM Summary, 2005/2006.

Report of the First Nations Cultural Heritage Impact Assessment and Consultation, Component: Bamberton Town Development Project. Website: http://www.racerocks.com/racerock/rreo/rrrefer/bamber/toc1.htm.

Shibley, Mark. "Sacred Nature: Earth-Based Spirituality as Popular Religion in the Secular Northwest." (Unpublished), Southern Oregon University, Ashland, Oregon.

Unitarian Church Information packet provided (it is presumed) by the Unitarian Church building committee or the board to proponents, for the design of the church, beginning "Part 1." (Courtesy Kate Gerson).

Yuquot Agenda Paper prepared by Mowachaht-Muchalaht First Nation for submission to Historic Sites and Monuments Board of Canada, 1997.

INDEX

ACKNOWLEDGEMENTS

IT MAY TAKE a village to raise a child, but it also seems to take a whole community of supporters and backstage promoters to give birth to a book. I've been lucky with my community, and I thank each person (and apologize to anyone I inadvertently overlook).

Beverley Sinclair, former editor of *Shared Vision* magazine, and Leslie Campbell and David Broadland, editor and publisher, respectively, of *Focus* Magazine, published my early pieces on sacred places. They gave me faith that people were interested in the subject.

Jennifer Breckon, curator of the Richmond Museum, shared helpful information about the Heritage of Faith: Spiritual and Sacred Places exhibit, held at the museum. I'd also like to acknowledge Marilyn Clayton at the museum; Bridget Coll and Ruth McIntosh at the Unitarian Church of Vancouver; Alex Fischer and Kate Carson, assistants to Robert Bateman; Erin McMillan of the Rick Hansen Foundation; Diane Switzer at the Vancouver Heritage Foundation and Karen Wootton at the Whistler Village Church. They all provided valuable assistance.

Margarita James and Juanita Amos helped to arrange my interviews at Yuquot. Chris Trehearne and Wendy Townsend assisted me at William Head Institution. Shaheen Tejani kindly verified information about the Burnaby Ismaili Jamatkhana. Deddeda Stemler helped out with photo preparation. And Farah Nosh made a special trip to Victoria to take my author photo. Thanks, Farah.

Several people read various drafts of chapters and helped with revisions, editing and their faith in the project. Thank you to Holly Broadland, Kristi Fuoco, Richard Inglis, Emily McClung, Dave Preston, Lesley Preston, Judy Slattery, Linette Smith, Suzanne Steele, Sid Tafler and especially to my husband, Russ Fuoco. Rod Weiss offered helpful suggestions and useful books. Both Rosemary Neering and the ever-patient Mark Zuehlke were more than generous with their advice, suggestions and authors' wisdom. And Jo-Ann Roberts provided her insights in her foreword.

◀ Star, Russ, Kristi and Holly on top of "Mount Live Forever" in 1987.

Bruce Lund told me I should go to Yuquot, if at all possible, and helped with contacts and information. Kate Gerson went beyond the call of duty to be sure I had her father's private letters and documents, and her sister Erika tracked down an old picture of Wolfgang Gerson for me—thank you.

For believing in my idea, even when I doubted it myself, I thank Murray Groom. I'd like to make note particularly of the Centre for Studies in Religion and Society (CSRS) at the University of Victoria, which selected me as a fellow so I could do research and work on this subject. When CSRS director Conrad Brunk encouraged me to apply for a fellowship, it was perhaps the first time I believed this book could and would happen. Thanks for your faith in the project.

I'd like to acknowledge the assistance of the Canada Council for the Arts, which supported my work through the Grants to Professional Writers: Creative Writing program. At that point, the idea went from possible to doable.

Thank you to Pat Touchie and Vivian Sinclair at TouchWood Editions, who have both been enthusiastic supporters from the start. The process was smoothed along by my editor, Marlyn Horsdal, who knows how to cut flab with the skill of a surgeon, while leaving the stuff that makes you look good; by Ruth Linka, who herded the project along with efficiency and dexterity, and by the whole TouchWood production, promotion and design team.

The artists and photographers who so willingly allowed the use of their work in the book all deserve special thanks. Joanne Thomson designed the beautiful chapter-head drawings, and Sue-Anne Carter was a lifesaver with manuscript formatting. Judy Slattery encouraged and gave advice to me throughout this long process, and was ever ready to read another draft. Linette and John Smith offered me the use of their cozy attic office. My family has always been there to support me, particularly Russ, who isn't afraid to tell me when something needs work, is always there to praise me when he thinks it's good and will read through draft after draft with hardly any complaining. He also cooks up irresistible meals to lure me out of my office cave at dinnertime.

Most of all, I'd like to acknowledge the storytellers, those generous people who make up this book and who so willingly told me stories of their sacred places. My deepest thanks to all those interviewed or quoted. What a thoughtful, fascinating group. You taught me to see how places are metaphors for that which is most important in our lives. These are your stories, and I thank you for sharing them.

STAR WEISS is an accomplished journalist, educator and author living in Victoria, BC. Her writing has appeared in the *Vancouver Sun*, *British Columbia Magazine*, the *Georgia Straight*, and *Harrowsmith*. This book is the culmination of her evolving spiritual beliefs and her lifelong interests in the outdoors and multiculturalism. To learn more about Star and her projects, visit http://www.starweiss.ca.